The Amazing Adventures of Captain Embers and Chief Zogleman; Whop, Whop, Whop

Helicopter pilots, 61st Assault Helicopter Co., LZ English, Bong Son, Vietnam, 1968-69

Checking the "Jesus nut", pre-flight inspection

Ken Embers

DEDICATION

Dedicated to the fine young men who served with the 61ˢᵗ Assault Helicopter Co., LZ English, Bong Son, Vietnam.

*Cover Photo: The "Jesus nut" secures the main rotor blade to the helicopter. It attaches the main rotor blade to the transmission mast.

CONTENTS

ACKNOWLEDGEMENTS

Thanks to Jim Sharp, WWII, Battle of the Bulge veteran and Sgt. of the Guard at the Nuremberg Trials for his advice and encouragement to complete these memoirs. To Curtis Kekahbah, Vietnam era Army veteran, Kaw Indian elder, and sweat lodge water pourer, for his eagerness to see this book in print. And, to all those who contributed to the 61st AHC Bong Son Lucky Star Blazer Library Learning Center, including my wife "Trish" for her personal support and for helping edit the manuscript.

For help with publishing, thanks to Tom Morrissey, artist, sculptor, professor of fine arts, especially Phil Marshall, author of 19 books on Helicopter Medivac Air Rescue missions in Vietnam, and Gary Roush, Editor & Chairman, Membership Directory, Vietnam Helicopter Pilots' Association, all Vietnam helicopter pilots.

And to Marlin Fitzwater, Presidential Spokesperson for both President H. W. Bush and President Ronald Reagan, author of *Call the Briefing* and other books, and college fraternity brother, my thanks for steering me in the right direction with the sage advice, "publishing is a learning experience".

Chapter 1. Night Extraction

Captain Embers strapped himself into the cockpit of a UH-1C helicopter gunship. Here we go again, another night mission in support of the 173rd Airborne Brigade LRRP's, the Long Range Reconnaissance Patrol team out in the An Lao valley. He cranked up the engine by flipping the battery switch on, main fuel switch on; check cyclic and pedals free play, roll throttle on the collective to detent mode, punch starter button, check N1 power to 40%, roll throttle full on and watched the rotor blades start to turn and listened to the whine of the jet turbine engine as it revved up to speed. All the instruments in the green, co-pilot, crew chief, door gunner all set. It was night in Vietnam, very dark, no lights in the countryside, no moonlight, no reference points to orient oneself. Couldn't even see the 2,000-foot mountains several miles west of LZ English nor the South China sea several kilometers to the east. Here we go, pull pitch by slightly raising the collective in your left hand, get light on the skids, push the cyclic in your right hand slightly forward, maintain direction with the foot pedals, slide out of the revetment, do a bouncing, skid-scraping, take-off run, hit translational lift where the whirling rotor blades achieve a flying wing-like status, and *we're airborne into the cool night air.*

Despite the danger and because of the adventure, Capt. Embers attempted to reassure himself by thinking, *"I'll be glad I did this when I get back to the States".*

The LRRP's were surrounded of course. The 6-man team had sprung an ambush on some night marauding V.C. and although they had killed some of the enemy, the V.C. survivors had radioed for help and were in hot pursuit of the American soldiers. One Lucky Star slick or troop ship had been assigned to pick up the team. Two Starblazer gunships were to cover the retrieval of the LRRP's. The LRRP team had called Lucky Ops, the operations office of the 61st Assault Helicopter Company, only minutes ago.

"We need to be picked up at these coordinates" the LRRP team radio man whispered.

"Why are you whispering?" said Lieutenant Briggs, Ops officer. *"We're surrounded"*, was the reply.

"OK, we'll be there in 10 minutes. Hold on, we're on the way."

"I wish these guys would spring ambushes on nice, bright, clear days, pre-plan the LZ location and give us a couple hours to prepare", thought Cpt. Embers, sardonically. LRRPs were specially trained Rangers who performed reconnaissance and disruptive attack missions against the enemy VC and NVA soldiers. The VC, Viet Cong, were the military arm of the National Liberation Front aligned with the NVA, North Vietnamese Army soldiers, who wanted to unify North and South Vietnam under a communist government.

The Lucky Star slick located the LRRP's using the map coordinates and homing in on them using FM radio. The LRRP team guided the helicopter in by saying, "Hey we hear your rotor blades and you're just to the east of us, come a little closer heading 270. OK, you're right over us, can you see the red tracer rounds going out?" And with no lights on the aircraft, no ground guide or lights on the ground, the Huey set down in a small clearing, having clipped a couple of palm tree fronds with its rotor blade while hovering into the extremely confined area. Green tracer fire followed the LRRPs as they plunged onto the UH-1D Huey. The Starblazer gunships fired back with mini-guns, 4,000 rounds per minute, and a couple of 2.75 in rockets to discourage the V.C. from further pursuit. The door gunner and crew chief fired back at the source of the green tracer rounds with their M-60 machine guns. "Let's go," yelled the crew chief, "we're up, all aboard!"

Chief Warrant Officer Zogleman calmly but firmly pulled pitch with the collective, came to a hover, pushed forward on the cyclic to nose over the aircraft and move forward, somehow found a clear lane to gain airspeed, achieve translational lift, and leapt into the sky. Well, those old D models didn't exactly leap into the sky with a full load and guns a-blazing, but the Chief being the consummate pilot that he was, avoiding trees, rocks, bushes, vines, anthills, and enemy fire, nursed it into the air and returned safely to LZ English. *Another successful mission accomplished*.

How did all this happen anyway? What led up to these circumstances and what were we, these two young men, and their many companions doing, 10,000 miles from home, in Vietnam?

Chapter 2. Dreams Can Come True!

Cpt. Embers, Ken, me, I watched as an airplane flew over the Kansas sky leaving an exhaust plume or contrail of white smoke. Wouldn't it be fun to be a pilot and go all over the world exploring new lands and people and places? It sure would, but here I am stuck on an old John Deere D tractor pulling a 3-bottom plow moving at 3 mph under a hot sun on a windy, dusty afternoon in the middle of Kansas. Things could be worse, after all, I've got a great family, parents, grandparents, small town, girlfriends sometimes, good friends, plenty to eat, sports activities, swimming, American Legion baseball, the YMCA and college in the future. *Yeah but....*

Several years later I graduated from college and joined the Army. My greatest fear upon graduation was that I would have to get a full-time job with regular hours. A degree in sociology, after changing majors from mechanical engineering and chemical engineering, didn't offer many exciting career opportunities, but fortunately Uncle Sam was there for me. *A chance to travel to foreign lands certainly beat a desk job, getting married, having kids and oh my god, settling down.*

The Army recruiter in Hutchinson, KS asked me if I'd like to go to Officer Candidate School. Sure, I replied, thinking that the girls in Officers' clubs were surely to be the prettiest of all and besides, as an officer I'd be able to make decisions on my own and have some control over my life. Ha Ha, although that was true to some extent, I was merely a cog in a much larger machine. Along with that came responsibility for the mission and your men while you, the officer, was third in the traditional military hierarchy of "mission, men, and me". *Accomplish the mission, take care of your men, and then worry about yourself,* the officer's creed.

Do you want to go into Ordinance, Logistics or the Engineers, asked the recruiter? No, I want to go into the Army, you know shooting stuff and all that. Oh, OK, combat arms, will it be the infantry, artillery or armor? Armor, what's that? Tanks. Yeah, I can drive a 1930 Model A Ford coupe, a tractor and a combine, so I'd like Armor. *A moving vehicle with guns, what a deal!*

The year was 1966 and my friends in my college fraternity were either getting married, joining the Air or Army National Guard or going to graduate school. All were effective draft avoidance and career enhancement pursuits at that time. My choice and several of my buddies chose the military, even though the Vietnam War was really getting hot and there was *some controversy over the best course for our country to take.*

Heck, John Wayne and Alan Ladd led the type of life in the military that looked more intriguing to me. Fly into danger and excitement, adventurous combat, foil the bad guys, rescue the fair young maiden and then return home to a rustic bar populated with exotic, dusky, almond-eyed, cinnamon skinned beauties with maybe Veronica Lake on the side. Besides, I was a good shot with a rifle and shotgun, loved the outdoors, played baseball and football, could run forever, was strong and reasonably intelligent. My Dad, a WWII Navy veteran, had mentioned the plight of C.O.'s, conscientious objectors, who wouldn't fight and were relegated to emptying bed pans during the war. Who'd want to do that? How inglorious.

Basic training was a blast. I was all alone at Ft. Bragg, NC. Didn't know a soul, but was assigned as squad leader, in charge of cleaning the latrines and picking up trash outside the old WWII barracks that we were housed in. *How was this different than being a C.O.?*

We learned all about marching, saluting, first aid, basic combat fighting, did a lot of Physical Training, jumping jacks, push-ups, squat jumps, up down, down up, hiked all over the sandy forested hills and spent nights out in the field in a "pup" tent with only a candle for heat. One little candle keeps a pup tent cozy in the mild winters of North Carolina.

At night, back in the barracks after "lights out" under the covers with a flashlight, I read Barbara Tuchman's book, *The Proud Tower: A Portrait of the World before the War, 1890-1914*, written in 1966, and another big book on the Black Death, the bubonic plague of the Middle Ages that killed 30-60% of the world population. There wasn't much to choose from in the Ft. Bragg PX, certainly not Bernard Fall's book *Street Without Joy*. That book nor any other book on the history of and what awaited us in Vietnam was available. Could this have been by design? The war in Vietnam was escalating and not going as planned by General Westmoreland, President Lyndon Johnson and Secretary of Defense Robert S. McNamara. How could a little ol' country that nobody had even heard of a few years ago be causing so much consternation? Westy kept asking for more troops, Mac compared the kill ratio in our favor, and LBJ sent them, resulting in a constant influx of troops that eventually reached 543,482 military personnel in Vietnam on 30 April, 1969.

Bernard Fall's book, *Street Without Joy,* described the perilous position of French troops in Vietnam in the 1950's and the pitfalls of fighting a guerilla force with a conventional military mind set. Exactly the problem that we would face in Vietnam. Nobody read it except the Green Berets. That knowledge and experience was ignored by the Americans who tried to model the construction of the South Vietnamese army, the Army of the Republic of Vietnam, the ARVN, after the type of force that was encountered in Korea, in the last war. The Americans built an ARVN military to fight frontal offensive attacks, but the VC and NVA used guerilla tactics to escape and evade after launching attacks when and where they chose to. *Not unlike the tactics that the American colonists used against the British in our Revolutionary War, circa 1776.*

The book on the bubonic plague attributed the Black Death to fleas on rats, which spread the disease to humans. It said that there were no deaths from the bubonic plague in prisons, 'cause the prisoners, always hungry, ate the rats, thus no fleas and no plague. A study I just read in 2022 said that theory was wrong. Too bad, I liked the part about the prisoners eating the rats. *Funny how the past changes depending on who's telling the story.*

We learned how to fire the new M-16 rifle. I didn't like it because it was plastic and didn't seem like a real gun. For some reason I wasn't a very good shot with it either, though I did get a marksmanship badge of some sort. "Wash and keep your mess kits clean after chow, not even greasy", said the first sergeant. Make your bed, keep things neat and tidy and at the end of 8 weeks it was off to AIT, Advanced Individual Training, at Ft. Knox, Kentucky.

 Hey this was even better; we got to drive M-48 tanks around. These monsters could go anywhere and were easy to drive, even had a steering wheel like a car but shaped a little oblong. In fact, they had automatic transmissions and zero-radius turning capabilities, just like expensive zero-turn lawn mowers of today. Inside was a mechanical computer, just line up the two images in the telescopic sight, place it on the target, choose an armor piercing or high explosive round and fire away. There was a big .50 caliber machine gun on top for the tank commander. Plus, crew members had a .45 caliber fully automatic "grease" gun and carried a .45 caliber automatic pistol. That was some fire power and we got familiarized with these weapons. That means we got to shoot them but didn't "qualify" with them.

I made some good friends in AIT at Ft. Knox. Platoon Sergeant Dixon always admonished us to get short hair cuts to keep us looking "neat and legible". One of my friends, who later became a lawyer, and I attended a showing of "Dr. Zhivago" on post at the old wooden theater. It was as cold and snowy inside the theater as it was in Russia in the movie, well almost. Another friend, an Irish kid and I, who were bunk mates, used to talk all the time. He said he loved the way Americans always had a response to something that somebody said and were able to come back with some jive or wise cracking comment.

One day after training I came back to our bunks and discovered that he was gone. Where did he go? No one knew. The Army had disappeared him. It reminded me of *Catch-22*, Joseph Heller's satirical WWII war novel, where weird things happen for no apparent reason. Another friend termed me the "philosopher" for some reason. He seemed well educated so I didn't question his reasoning and was actually pleased with the moniker.

So just like that it was off to Armor Officer Candidate School for six months. Oops, this weren't no bull shit boys! These guys were out for blood, this was the real thing. We were harassed and belittled to no end. Fortunately, I had gone through pledge training in a college fraternity, and although this was much much more in depth and continuous, I knew the program and being a resilient young man could handle the pressure with a secret smile. The training was very thorough. We learned how to read contour maps in detail. I could tell what terrain features were coming up as we drove our tanks through unfamiliar terrain and knew how to look for ambushes. We were taught how to operate, disassemble, clean and reassemble rifles, machine guns, radios and do field repairs on tanks and armored personnel carriers. Even how to hook tanks up to trees to pull themselves out of mud holes and over rough terrain.

We ran everywhere, always singing and chanting something like, "I wanta be an airborne ranger, I wanta live a life of danger". It felt good to be in good shape, I even had a small waist and a "V" type upper body image when I looked in the mirror. The food was good, though we had to sit at attention and eat "square" meals. Square meals in OCS are when you lift your fork from your plate to your mouth at a 90-degree angle while looking straight ahead and never eyeballing or looking directly at the person across from you. Oh, we shined our boots and brass and learned how to make a bed so tight that a quarter would bounce off it. We also kept the latrines spic and span sometimes using toothbrushes on the floor around the edges of the stools. OCS was a great combination of physical and mental exercise that taxed even the best and brightest. Some didn't make it and washed out. The physical training and mental pressure were intense and seemed pointless at times, so it tested your perseverance and stamina.

One disturbing thought troubled me. One day when we were training in tactics, we were at a mockup of a hill defended by the enemy and we, the good guys, were supposed to capture the hill. After some deliberation, the Tactical Officer announced that the best solution would result in a loss of only 15% of our good guys. Hmmm, what if I were in that 15%? *I thought that surely there must be a better solution to these conflicts.*

And then there was the time when the instructor, a seasoned Army Officer, posed the question: "What if you're surrounded by the enemy, they are bearing down on you, what would you do?" Too late, he said that if you had to think about it, then you would die. *An officer had to respond immediately, right or wrong, you, the Lieutenant, had to do something.*

So, one day while we were standing in formation, it was announced to us that, "Any person desiring to go to helicopter flight school should report to building X for the vision test in two days". I immediately took off my glasses, which I used sometimes for far away vision like night driving and practiced my long-distance vision for the next two days. I never read a book or let my eyes focus up close. I wanted to pass that test and get into flight school. I'd never thought about flying helicopters, only airplanes. Since I didn't pass the Navy flight school vision test, I had joined the Army, figuring a two-year stint after OCS was better than 4 years in the Navy.

On the appointed day I arrived at the gymnasium where the testing was taking place. "Embers, you're next." They put some drops in my eyes and told me to wait, which I did while focusing my eyes on the red exit sign at the other end of the gymnasium. Next candidate was me. I got up, keeping my eyes focused for distance, sat down, and read the eye chart as requested.

"Ok you pass, next", announced the specialist examiner.

I got up from the chair and walked out of the room thinking, "What have I got myself into now?" A couple of weeks later I had my orders for flight school. Yippee, I had always wanted to fly! Ever since my Grandad Bird had taken me to the McPherson airport and let me sit at the controls of a J-3 Cub when I was 4 or 5 years old.

After 6 months of training in OCS, I received my commission as a 2nd Lieutenant with assignment to the 7th of the 1st Air Cav. They were preparing to go to Vietnam and my flight school class didn't start for a couple of months. I became a training officer and was in charge of completing all the training records of the Head Quarters company. I dutifully if somewhat reluctantly filled in, by hand, all the records and had them ready for inspection, which never came. In December of '67, as the 7/1 Cav was departing for Vietnam and I was leaving for flight school, the First Sergeant, a not so gentle giant, gleefully informed me that all my records would be dumped in the Dempster Dumpster. There were parts of the Army that I didn't like.

Then in January of 1968, after a vacation skiing in Colorado with fraternity brothers who had joined the Air Force and Air Guard, I reported for flight school and duty at Ft. Wolters, in Mineral Wells, TX. This was a big change. I now lived in the Baker Hotel, doubled up with another lieutenant to save money, and was assigned to the Gray hats, a bunch of newly commissioned 2nd Lieutenants wanting to learn to fly helicopters .

I had what I thought was a rather old man, maybe early to mid-forties as a civilian flight instructor. He had been a bomber pilot in WWII and could see better than I could. One day in the early stages of training, he said, "You've got traffic, a helicopter, at 9 o'clock." I wasn't able to see it, so I went into Ft. Worth and got some prescription sun glasses that looked just like Army aviator sunglasses. No one knew that I was wearing prescription lens. I wondered what would happen at the end of flight school and I would probably have to take another vision test.

Once again military training was thorough and timely. Ground school and introduction to flying, weather conditions and forecast, map reading, safety procedures and how to fly the Hiller OH-23 was a really exciting time. Oh, I forgot to mention my fear of heights. Yes, it seems that as a kid I fell out of a tree and had to go the doctor for a hernia or hemorrhage that the doctor said I would grow out of. I did but I still didn't like heights. Fortunately, *my desire to fly, exceeded my fear of heights* and flying came to be like riding on a motorcycle. It's OK if you are in control, but not so good if you're on the back seat.

Flying was fascinating. So many factors influence the flight of an airplane or helicopter. The history of aviation and of the bold pioneers of aviation, is spellbinding. How did those guys make it work, and the helicopter, once diagrammed by Leonardo Da Vinci, finally came into being shortly before WWII. At last, the materials were strong enough, the engine small, light and powerful enough and the technology advanced enough to get that contraption off the ground and into the air. Remarkable!

When I first got up close to a helicopter, an OH-23, observation helicopter, in flight school with my instructor, I stared in awe at the little machine. It wasn't as big as a wheat harvest combine. And we were going to fly that thing! We got in, the instructor cranked it up. It shook, rattled and rolled from side to side. The pulleys, levers, gears, and belts all hummed and whirred. Why I can do this, I thought.

This is just like a combine but instead of a header bar and a reel out front, it has rotor blades overhead. This is going to be fun.

But another thought crept into my head. You know, I could bring down this aircraft with a .22 rifle. Just shoot the pilot who is easily visible in the plexiglass bubble. Or shoot the rotor mechanism or punch a hole in the gas tank. Never the less, this was flying and I had dreamed of it ever since those days plowing in the Kansas wheat fields.

Hovering was a big challenge. Just pull up on the collective lever with your left hand. This increases the pitch, or angle of attack, in the rotor blades, and roll on the throttle like on a motorcycle, lifting you up and down. Using your right hand on the cyclic stick between your legs, guide the aircraft left to right, forward to backward. Keep the nose pointed in the direction you want to go with your feet by pushing the two pedals in front of you. This changes the pitch in the tail rotor blades and turns the aircraft left or right. Try to keep it over one spot at 3 feet off the ground. Not so easy the first time, but eventually you learn to make those micro movements of hand-eye-feet coordination that keep you in position. Now nose over the aircraft, i.e., tilt the rotor forward with the cyclic, increase the power by rolling on the throttle located on the collective, pull up on the collective, maintain direction with your feet on the pedals, hit translational lift at about 15 knots airspeed, and poof, just like magic, you are slowly climbing and sailing up into the sky.

Not everybody got the hang of hovering and the more advanced maneuvers like autorotating to the ground with engine cut to idle. It's quite a skill to be able to land a helicopter after the engine accidently quits. We practiced it methodically, just in case. It's an art to be able to set it down on a spot with no forward air speed and not damage the helicopter, but we got pretty good at it. Helicopter pilots don't wear parachutes, so it was imperative to develop this skill. For four and half months we learned how to fly, navigate cross country, night or day, land in confined areas. All of this after we had soloed, or flown by ourselves around the traffic pattern and then on cross countries and into confined areas. A confined area is a spot on the ground out on the Texas plains that has been designated as an area to practice landing to pick up troops or material, our soon to be mission in Vietnam.

If you couldn't develop these skills in the time allotted, then you would be recycled to a class behind yours and given a chance to succeed a second time, usually. If you couldn't get it by then or were a hazard to aviation, then you were dropped from flight school. The wash out rate was high in some classes, 10-30%, and we had a few, but most made it through primary helicopter school. It was probably harder for the Warrant Officer Candidates who were living in barracks and undergoing conditioning harassment from their cadre of Warrant Officers while also learning to fly. But once you soloed, oh boy, what a feeling.

Chapter 3. Mother Rucker

The drive to my next assignment at Fort Rucker, Alabama, was beautiful and refreshing. In my little red VW beetle, I cruised along the highway viewing the beautiful spring flowers of east Texas, Mississippi and Alabama. Ft. Rucker, the Home of Army Aviation and helicopter flight school was full of aspiring helicopter pilots and seasoned instructors who had been to Vietnam and returned. It was affectionately called "Mother Rucker" by some enthusiasts.

I lived in a mobile home trailer in Enterprise, Alabama, with another lieutenant and drove to work every day. The training was once again rigorous and thorough. Now we had to learn how to fly on instruments, or in the blind, with no visual references. Using the OH-13 helicopter, like the one you see in episodes of Mash on TV, we placed a shield over our eyes so that we, the student pilots, couldn't see outside the cockpit but only had reference to the gauges on the dash board panel. Oh my, this was a challenge! You had to believe the gauges, the altimeter that told your height above sea level, the air speed indicator, turn and bank indicator, compass, attitude indicator, vertical speed indicator and navigational radios, the ADF and VOR pointer needles to figure out where you were. And, you had two other radios, FM and VHF, to talk to the controllers and other aircraft. Quite a lot of information in addition to monitoring the engine instruments.

Sometimes you felt like you were turning, when you weren't. The inner ear plays tricks on you when you don't have visual references to augment your balance information. You had to concentrate and believe the instruments, not your physical sensations. A mastery of mind over matter that all instrument rated pilots must acquire. You get better at it the more you do it. We practiced appropriate radio procedures and safety precautions while flying in the high-density traffic of the training area.

Then we got to transition into the UH-1 Huey helicopter. This was a tremendous upgrade in power and flying capabilities from the small reciprocating engine aircraft we had been flying. Those other aircraft with their small underpowered engines, why they could barely kill you. *Pilot humor.*

 The Huey had a jet turbine engine, could carry 10 people, fly for a couple of hours or more and had a synchronized throttle linked to the collective which made control more positive and stable. *Everybody loved the Huey.*

I still had a problem concerning the final vision test before I would be awarded my wings. One day after flying, and on the bus back from a stage field, my buddy and I were doing the cross-word puzzle in the Army Times. I saw an article which said: "Any aviator or flight school candidate whose vision is correctable to 20/20 is eligible for flight status". Hurray, the Army in all its wisdom had changed the regulations and I was going to be able to complete my flight training and get my wings. Just in time because a couple of weeks later I was called for the final vision test.

I went in and set down. Lt. Embers, sir, I was a "sir" now, not a hey you, would you like to take your test now. Maybe they weren't that polite, but anyway, I tried to read the chart without my secret prescription aviator sunglasses and the examiner said, "Sir, you won't be able to receive your wings as your vision has dimmed since the last test". They didn't know about the change in the Army Regulations, it was that new. So I gladly informed the examiners that I would need two pairs of clear glasses and two pairs of sunglasses, because I already had my orders for Vietnam and the regs had changed. Then I had 30 days leave before I left for my great adventure that I had always wanted. A trip to a new and strange land, and flying!

Two of my fraternity brothers contacted me when they heard that I was on my way to Vietnam. They urged me to come on out to San Francisco for a week and enjoy life, (before death in Vietnam?). I gladly accepted the invitation. But first I had to go to Ft. Riley, KS, and get my ticket. I was going economy class from San Francisco to Saigon with a stop in Honolulu, Hawaii, on the way.

Thinking ahead, I asked the Army specialist on duty at the travel point at Ft. Riley to give me a round trip ticket to and back from Vietnam. With a slight smirk and hint of humor, he dryly noted that my return ticket would be issued after a year in Vietnam and prior to my return.

My two fraternity brothers had a nice old, two-story Victorian house on a corner in a hilly section of San Francisco. They had arranged for a series of occasions, dinners, parties, restaurants, dancing in clubs, and picnics with some girlfriends. One in particular took a liking to me, and I to her, probably she had agreed to be my date for this whirlwind week.

One day we traveled across the Golden Gate Bridge and had a picnic in a meadow on the side of a hill looking back towards the Bridge and San Francisco. The view was breath-taking, the company fabulous, the food tasty and the red wine intoxicating. White puffy clouds sailed across the blue sky as ships and tug boats passed under the bridge and tooted their joy of being alive. This was what I always remembered when things weren't just right in Vietnam and I needed to remember what I was fighting for and why. I wanted an America that brimmed with happiness and opportunity to do whatever I wanted with good people, like the ones I was with. *This vision sustained me through my year abroad.*

On the night of my departure to Vietnam, I suited up in my khaki uniform. I was a 1st Lieutenant, Armor branch, with a pair of wings on my chest, a good conduct medal and my marksmanship badge. All set for new adventures. As we left the house there was a casually dressed long haired young man in jeans and a tie-dyed T-shirt on the corner looking through a telescope. He saw me and said, "Hey man, you wanna take a look?" He offered me a view of the vast planetary expanse and offered a comment to the effect that, "There is a lot going on out there, isn't there?". I took a look through the telescope, saw some stars, galaxies and planets and agreed that there sure was a lot going on out there.

We arrived at the SFO airport. Only my two buddies accompanied me. My "girl" didn't show up as she professed not being good at saying good-bye. I picked up my duffel bag, said thanks for a wonderful time and headed for the terminal. Before I entered the building I bent down and kissed the ground. I'll be back I intoned to the earth. I was already using some kind of sympathetic magic designed to insure my safe return.

The plane stopped in Honolulu and we were given an hour to walk about while the plane refueled. I headed for the bar and downed a couple of Mai Tai's. We could have walked out the front gate and disappeared into the Hawaiian hills if so inclined, but the thought never entered my mind, hardly.

Chapter 4. Pearl of the Orient:

Arriving in Saigon at night, we were greeted by green tracer rounds arching up into the sky. The Viet Cong enemy used green tracer rounds; we used red ones. Every fifth bullet would be a tracer round so the shooter could see where the bullets were going. That also meant that the person being shot at could trace the bullet back to its source. I always thought that we, the good guys, should have the green tracer rounds, while the communist enemy, the reds, should use red tracer rounds. *This was one of the many enigmas that graced the conflict.*

The door popped open and the hot humid smell of Saigon, Vietnam, greeted us as we descended the metal staircase plunging us into the midst of a motley crew of dirty, disheveled, returning G.I.'s whose year was up and they were returning to the U.S.

"You'll be sorry," they yelled encouragingly. I descended the gangway and sought out a restroom.

"Where's the latrine?" Someone pointed to a low one-story small building and I entered into a quagmire of over flowing stools of piss and shit all over the floor. Stepping gingerly through the muck I relieved myself and got out of there as quickly as possible.

We were then loaded onto a bus with chicken wire netting covering all the windows. "That's to stop anyone from throwing in a grenade", the driver said reassuringly. I was starting to withdraw into myself thinking that this wasn't a very well-planned reception for new troops and wondering who was in charge here. *No one ever seemed to be really in charge nor had anyone really thought out what was going on and done something about it.*

The next day I and a couple of guys that I didn't know were assigned to board a helicopter to Nha Trang and on to our future assignments. The view from the helicopter was of a beautiful green land, low mountains covered with trees, the sparkling blue South China sea, and shining white sand beaches. This place is gorgeous, I thought. *"We should be doing business here instead of having a war."*

Upon landing at the airport, we were guided to a two-story hootch. "You are on the second floor, pick out a bunk and you'll be notified of your future assignments." The building was nice and clean with wood siding and window screen on all sides. Open air sleeping with ceiling fans to circulate the air. The second floor sounds good to me, up off the ground and away from snakes and anyone that might want to disturb us.

I went up the outside wooden staircase and opened the second-floor door. There were 10 or so single layer bunk beds on each side of the open bay. Let's see which would be most restful and out of the way in case of an untimely entrance by an enemy intruder who might want to do me harm. Aha, I'll go to the far end, away from the door. But wait, there is no way out on that end, and I don't want to be right beside the entrance door, so I'll choose that bed on the right side in the middle of all the others. As I headed for my chosen bunk the rotating ceiling fan above the bed broke loose and came crashing down in the middle of the bed. *That's not a good omen.* A rotating blade falls out of the sky and I'm a helicopter pilot. I chose a different bed.

Eventually I was assigned to the 61st Assault Helicopter Company stationed at LZ English near the little village of Bong Son. Scuttlebutt was that of the 4 companies in the 268th Battalion, the one you didn't want was the 61st AHC at English. They were kind of the bastard child of the 268th BN, didn't have nice accommodations like showers and an officers' club, or a maintenance facility adjoining the unit.

Chapter 5. LZ English

It was an overcast dreary day when I arrived in the back of a helicopter and landed on the Crap Table, the oiled landing strip used to park, refuel, and reload helicopters of the 61st. The 61st AHC logo was a pair of dice with the six and the one showing so the "Crap Table" was an apt description, an appropriate and thoughtful name for our home port.

There were some pluses that I read into being assigned to this "orphan" company permanently assigned to occupy a temporary position supporting the 173rd Airborne Brigade. The call sign of the 61st slicks or troop lift ships was the "Lucky Stars". Now that was a good name and augmented well and then again 6 plus 1 equals 7, a lucky number, and I had graduated from high school in '61 and my football jersey number was 61, all good. *I had never been superstitious before, but now it seemed I was searching for some reassuring landmarks.*

"Where you from", asked one of the pilots. Kansas, I replied and he said that, oh, you'll want to meet Zogleman, he's from El Dorado, Kansas. Another reassuring factor, if a guy from Kansas was here too then, well what the heck, this was going to work out. My Mom's side of the family had relation in El Dorado so I had cousins that lived there.

Zog, Mike Zogleman, Chief Zogleman, the guy from Burns, a little town near El Dorado, showed me around the camp and introduced me to the warrant officers who lived in GP medium tents. I smiled and laughed naively as one of the W-1's declared that they had running water and pointed to a rivulet running through the dirt floor of their tent. It was the beginning of the monsoon season. Later, an extra duty of mine was to secure lumber and materials to build screened-in hootches with raised wooden floors for the warrants and the enlisted men.

I was given a small single room in a relatively nice ramshackle wooden hootch with screens for windows and walls built of left-over 2.75" rocket and 7.62 mini-gun, and M-60 machine gun ammo crate wood. It seems the commissioned officers had taken it upon themselves to build more genteel quarters up off the ground while assuring the non-commissioned warrant officers that they could do the same thing if they desired. The latter never happened and was a constant source of complaint among the warrants that the RLO's, "real live officers" had reneged on their promise of building such luxurious accommodations for them after they had helped the RLO's build their hootches from the ammunition crate wood and other scrounged materials. The roof leaked when it rained, which was often, but it was nice to have a wooden floor and a kerosene lamp to read by at night and to write an occasional letter to my San Francisco "girl," the folks and a buddy or two.

I was assigned to the first lift platoon, 8 UH-1D and H model helicopters. The H's were newer models with more powerful gas turbine jet engines. There were two platoons of slicks, the troop and supply lift ships, and one platoon of UH-1C gunships. The gunship platoon call sign was the Starblazers. Now who ever came up with these names was a creative genius. Later I found that the first company commander's nickname had been "Lucky" and the pilots had all submitted names. One of them came up with Lucky Stars and the company commander had liked it, and another wag had facetiously thrown in the Star Blazers for the guns, which was really quite fortuitous and fitting.

I was given an in-country check ride by the unit SIP, Standardization Instructor Pilot, a CW2, chief warrant officer who had demonstrated superior flying skills and knowledge of the helicopter. Warrant officers were almost always the best most dedicated pilots. Their sole mission was to fly the helicopter and they were very good at it. We did some take offs and landings, a couple of auto-rotations to the ground, checked out the landmarks, like the South China sea to the east, the An Lao and Sui Cau valleys and mountains to the west, and An Lao River which ran through the An Lao Valley, and the Bong Son bridges.

There were two bridges, one built earlier by the French and used for a railroad. It had been blown up and another for vehicular traffic was on Highway 1, the only connecting road from Saigon to Hanoi. There wasn't much traffic on the 2-lane black top; hardly any except for a military vehicle now and then.

I started flying missions as a PIC, pilot in command. The AC, aircraft commander was in charge of the aircraft and the mission. The AC was the seasoned veteran of several months and despite his rank, his word was followed. One night after I had just arrived and was an anxiety-filled guy, I was assigned to be a slick co-pilot on standby "scramble missions."
If a friendly unit got into trouble, they could call for air support and we would come to the rescue, either extracting them from their position, or providing covering fire. The most demanding mission was to land in an unmarked, unlit jungle area with enemy troops in the vicinity firing on our guys, at night, with no moonlight.

About midnight the call comes. "Embers, scramble mission, report to the TOC (tactical operations center)." I'm peacefully writing a letter by the light of my kerosene lantern, so I grab my maps, aviator helmet, strap on my .38 Smith and Wesson revolver, grab my chicken plate (bullet proof chest protector) and nervously head out the door. From a nearby room one of the pilots is playing "Bridge Over Troubled Waters", by Simon and Garfunkle, on a TEAC 4010 S reel to reel tape deck. I listen to the refrain, "like a bridge over troubled waters, I'll be there for you...". Gee I'd like to be back in the states, sitting around with some friends, I think. Instead, I'm heading out for a dangerous mission on a pitch-dark night, when one of the pilots sitting around, not on duty, drinking a beer, hollers at me, as I prepare to leave, "Hey Embers, if you don't come back, can I have your electric fan". An electric fan was a god send, when and if we had electricity. I didn't think the comment was funny at the time, in fact I gulped, turned white and felt a sickening sensation in my stomach, but in retrospect that was probably the funniest thing that ever happened to me in Vietnam. Good ole dark combat humor.

Then began a series of missions supporting the 173rd Airborne Brigade Sky Soldiers, originally airborne paratroopers, who jumped out of planes like on D-Day in WWII. The unit performed the only mass air assault in Vietnam in Operation Junction City in 1967. The 173rd Head Quarters was now at LZ English, a large Landing Zone with a small airstrip capable of landing C-130 Air Force planes and the temporary home of the 61st AHC.

With the advent of helicopters, we airlifted the Sky Soldiers to the battlefield and resupplied them with ammunition, food and supplies. They had a couple of helicopters assigned to them for command and control but the 61st AHC provided mission support. The 173rd had been in Vietnam since 1965 and had fought hard bloody battles with the North Vietnamese forces at Dak To and many other locations in South Vietnam. Their mission now was to prevent the North Vietnamese Army, the PAVN, People's Army of Vietnam, the communists, from splitting South Vietnam into two parts and taking over the central highland and coastal areas. This area was called II Corps and included Quy Nhon, An Khe, Kon Tum, up to Duc Pho and Quang Ngai. Quang Ngai was in I Corps and was near the scene of the infamous My Lai Massacre that occurred March

16, 1968 about one year before I was appointed gunship platoon leader.

We were not involved in this incident, thank God, and I never heard about it until after returning to the States. I couldn't believe it at first. We never did anything like that. In fact, the 173rd's mission had just been changed from "search and destroy", to "winning the hearts and minds of the Vietnamese people", though the 173rd had not been trained for such a mission and were revising their tactics.

The My Lai Massacre was when troops of the American Division stationed near Duc Pho were tasked with eliminating NVA/VC action in a fertile agricultural area not far from the sea coast.

More than a month earlier, during the Tet Offensive of 1968, the VC/NVA had taken over the Citadel Headquarters in Hue and the radio station. To eliminate South Vietnamese resistance the VC/NVA rounded up, tortured and killed over 4,000 military and civilian administrators who had cooperated with the Americans.

The units of the American had been harassed by guerrilla warfare of booby traps and sniper fire for weeks. They were never able to engage the enemy in a conventional set-piece battle, which they would have surely won since we, the Americans, had superior artillery fire power, air power, and coastal fire power from the Navy. The American soldiers had been losing men constantly and were eager to inflict losses on the rascals causing them so much hurt.

So when the General asked the Colonel what the hell was going on, why was he losing men and not killing the enemy, the Colonel indicated his desire for revenge to the Major, who then relayed it to the Captain, who then pumped up the Lieutenant by remonstrating that anyone who supported the NVA/VC were the enemy and that McNamara's War, this war, was about body count, all hell broke loose. The Americal soldiers entered a small village in the area and unlike the usual practice of befriending the villagers, the highly emotional soldiers ripped apart the straw homes in search of weapons, food and supplies that the villagers might aid the VC. Any Vietnamese that ran away was shot. Then even the women, old men and children, were herded into a ditch and shot. Some 400 civilians were killed. Not all of the American soldiers took part in this dastardly deed.

This malfeasance was stopped by Hugh Thompson, a warrant officer OH-23 helicopter pilot. He landed, confronted Lt. Calley, the infantry platoon leader, and flew some of the wounded Vietnamese to medical help. A big cover-up ensued but eventually this atypical atrocity was recognized and the perpetrators punished, but not severely. As a result, Vietnam veterans were called "baby killers".

On our first return trip to Vietnam in 2009, we encountered a young Vietnamese man in an outdoor café, adjacent to the train station, in Quy Nhon whose uncle had been an NVA soldier and we talked about these incidents. His comment was, *"It was war, men become animals and do crazy things."*

The Vietnamese peasant was put in quite a quandary. By day the Americans ruled the roads and roamed through the villages. By night, the NVA/VC crept into the villages and asked for, demanded, food and supplies. They also recruited by force, if necessary, the young men of the village to fight on their side. Some of the Vietnamese village young men went willingly, convinced that throwing out the foreign invaders was a righteous effort.

I noticed that the average farmer-peasant just wanted to be left alone. One time when we were inserting combat troops into an area which included some rice paddies, I saw an elderly farmer dressed as usual in grey black pajamas with a conical hat just standing on a small dike and ignoring the action going on around him as he tended his fields. Helicopters were landing, troops were exiting the air craft and running to the tree lines, gunships were strafing the jungle cover and here was this guy going about his business as usual. It struck me that this guy wished that both the Americans and NVA/VC would all just go home and leave him alone.

Ho Chi Minh had a well thought-out propaganda program in place for encouraging the Vietnamese people to expel the imperialistic Americans from their homeland. He and General Giap, the brilliant military strategist and former school teacher, equated the Americans to the colonialist French who had over-powered the former rulers of Vietnam and had proceeded to mine the wealth of the empire. The French were your typical European overlords and treated the Vietnamese as heathens being saved by the more advanced Christian nations of the West.

Remember Pope Alexander the VI who in 1493 issued the "Doctrine of Discovery". This 'License to Kill' essentially said that "All territories not under control of the Catholic Church are subject to the rule of the European Christian nations, etc., and the more advanced, civilized countries were authorized by Holy Roman writ to do as they pleased to control, educate and use the new lands in a way most profitable to the cause of Christendom.

Well, Vietnam had been colonized by the French since 1877. Sure lots of progress and advances in mining, logging, and agriculture had developed and millions of the Vietnamese had adopted the French language and the Roman Catholic religion. But Ho Chi Minh was the smartest, internationally experienced, strongest, and most ruthless leader of the several disparate groups that wanted to wrest control of the government from the foreign invaders and unite the country as an independent entity and sovereign nation. Whose side would you be on if you were Vietnamese? I started wondering about the justification for our presence in Vietnam.

As a young South Vietnamese person, you had two choices in 1954 following the Geneva Accords: you could follow the newly formed National Liberation Front and fight for the unification of Vietnam under a communist regime, or join the South Vietnamese

Army and fight for a non-communist separate South Vietnam. The Geneva Accords called for a nationwide election to determine if the country was to be unified under North Vietnam's communist government or South Vietnam's democratic regime. There was lots of confusion, mistrust and animosity at the conference. Russia and China, North Vietnam's allies loomed in the background. In fact, the concerned parties wouldn't even meet, shake hands and talk directly to each other. The U.S. and South Vietnam didn't feel that the election results would be in their favor, so they refused to participate in the election process. The Geneva Accords were a diplomatic failure on both sides. It was at this time that the U.S. started its ill-fated journey of "helping" South Vietnam resist communism. We, the U.S. wanted to help the South Vietnamese have freedom of speech, a democracy, a capitalist system, voting rights, freedom of religion and all the benefits of our American system.

The U.S. decided to help South Vietnam build an army of Vietnamese soldiers to protect themselves from the evil atheistic communists who would control and manipulate the South Vietnamese populace. However, the U.S. built an army in its own image, an army designed to fight overt battles with set-piece artillery and front lines, like they had just fought in Korea in the early 1950's. This army was ill suited to the guerrilla warfare that ensued and was not able to adapt to the tremendous onslaught of sustained attacks by the V.C. and NVA. Although initially successful on many fronts, the South Vietnamese army, the ARVN, Army of the Republic of Viet Nam, was seen as an extension of the old French sponsored, Army of Vietnam. *This meant that the ARVN was seen as representing a colonial power and was not an indigenous military force. It didn't have the moral justification of defending the common people of Vietnam, just a defense force for the already established wealthy and important segment of the upper strata of Vietnamese society.*

Many days and nights were spent flying those wonderful Hueys all over the II Corps area of South Vietnam. Our crew chiefs kept those helicopters in top shape considering that our maintenance facility was located in An Son at LZ Lane near Quy Nhon. It was an hour's flight to get there, but the 61st was able to provide more immediate support to the 173rd by stationing helicopters, unofficially, at LZ English rather than flying out of Lane Army Heliport, miles away.

Several helicopter crews had been lost when the unit first arrived in Vietnam. Not being used to flying in the monsoon season and unfamiliar terrain caused accidents and mishaps, such as flying into the side of a mountain and getting lost never to be seen again. Chief Zogleman told me that it was rumored that our unit was derisively called the "Falling Stars" instead of the "Lucky Stars." In any case, the unit was now a close-knit band of survivors and seasoned veterans. That is until the year was up. The tour of duty for an American soldier was one year. If you survived for one year, you got to go home! So, the point was to spend your year and go home. *Not win the war and go home, which would have given extra incentive to reconcile the differences.*

To preclude everyone in the unit from all going home at the same time, newly arrived replacement individuals were infused into each company and former members were sent to different companies. I arrived in October of 1968. The 61st had come in country about a year before and thus most of the pilots were due to soon go home, leaving the new guys and infused personnel to carry on. This led to some confusion and a loss of history of lessons learned. Sometimes we landed in LZ's and took enemy fire. Every time the company had landed there before they had taken fire. There was a lack of company history and communication that resulted from this replacement idea. In future wars, the U.S. abandoned this policy and now sends units that have trained together into battle instead of replacing individuals and leaving the unit in name.

Some of our most harrowing missions were the LRRP, Long Range Reconnaissance Patrol missions, as previously noted, but there were many other combat operations that showed the skill and daring of individuals dedicated to doing the best they could. Due to the bad weather during the monsoon season, October to February in our area, it rained a lot, the clouds hung low, visibility was reduced and helicopter support and flying in general became problematic.

One day when a LRRP team was in deep danger, being chased by NVA and their dogs, they called into

Lucky Operations for extraction. "We need to get out of here, can you send someone." No one wanted to go. It was the monsoon season. It was impossible, visibility was severely limited in the area. It was in the mountains.

Warrant Officer Sam Kyle stepped forward. "I'll go", he said. I put them in there, I know where they are, I'll give it a try". His crew volunteered to go with him and off they went, flying low and slow, barely seeing the palm trees and forest below until they came to the low range of mountains to the west. Looking out the side window and lower plexiglass bubble down between his feet, he hovered up the side of the mountain. The crew chief on his side closely watched for obstacles as they slowly ascended the side of the mountain until they reached an outcropping of rock, a small cliff protruding from the mountainside but not big enough to set the helicopter down on.
"We can hear your rotor blades and we are coming towards you, radioed the LRRP team. We are just about out of ammo." Dogs could be heard barking in the background as the NVA chased the LRRP's.

"I see someone," yelled the crew chief, he could dimly make out a figure through the driving rain. All six of the LRRP's jumped aboard and Sam slowly descended down the side of the mountain and then flew back to LZ English. The skill, technique, crew coordination and concentration that went in to doing this is a testament to the character and training of some fine young men. When they got back to English the LRRP team leader said to Sam, "thanks for the ride, Sir" and walked off into the mist. *Now these guys were brave, no doubt about it.*

Helicopters were occasionally shot up in the LZ, abandoned, the crew extracted by another helicopter crew and reinforcements were brought in to secure the area. A big heavy-lift twin-rotor Chinook helicopter would come and airlift the downed Huey for repair.

Wounded 173rd soldiers were evacuated by Dust Off, the medivac helicopters that were called in for that specific duty. Sometimes when they weren't available, we would haul out wounded or dead soldiers. It was an eerie feeling to know that death lurked so nearby. I didn't like to look back at the carnage in my helicopter, besides it was distracting.

I realized that this was dangerous business. I had a 50/50 chance of surviving in a way. The way I looked at it was that I could either get shot down, and there wasn't much I could do about that, or I might have an accident, flying helicopters in this environment was highly risky business. I wonder if more pilots were killed inadvertently due to the hazardous nature of the job than to enemy fire in combat. I decided that I could do something about the former and decided to devote myself to being the best pilot I possibly could be, paying attention at all times and doing the right thing.

Don't panic, was my motto. If things go awry, evaluate, choose the best option and don't forget to breathe. It worked pretty well. Early on, I did have to autorotate to a rice paddy when the engine quit when we were returning from a mission in the highlands. I was the co-pilot since I was new, but I noticed that the 20-minute fuel remaining warning light had come on, and the right fuel boost warning light had come on. It's not good when your instrument panel starts lighting up with red lights. I warned the Aircraft Commander, one of the seasoned warrants that had been there maybe six months that I remembered from flight school that if your right fuel boost pump is out and your low on fuel, you should put the helicopter down, land immediately, as you would soon run out of fuel.

"I'm not so sure about that," the AC pilot intoned. Right about then, the engine quit! Holy Shit, I thought, if this guy doesn't know that then I'm sure he'll need some help in this autorotation and landing to the ground. So I did what you're not supposed to do; I grabbed the cyclic and collective and "guided" us to a landing in a rice paddy while radioing on the emergency frequency our location as we descended. Our logical landing spot happened to be right on the tracks of the one railroad in the country that went from north to south, so rather than get our skids caught in the tracks, we extended our glide by nosing over the aircraft. And, then to zero out the air speed so that we could land in a rice paddy filled with water, we pulled back on the cyclic which dropped our tail rotor into the water, thrusting us forward up on to the chin bubble, which broke and spewed water all over the cock pit. But just as the tail was rising to flip the helicopter head over heels, it settled back into the rice paddy right side up. We had 3 or 4, 173rd guys in back with a .50 caliber machine gun and ammo. Their weight had helped hold us down. They jumped out and set up a perimeter. I meanwhile was frantically clawing at the armor plate between me and the door to my right side and trying to exit the helicopter before it burst into flames.

"We aren't on fire" the AC said as he tapped my arm. Sure enough, we weren't, we had made it down safely if somewhat crudely. The helicopter was OK, except for the chin bubble and maybe a hole where the right fuel boost pump had been shot out. I pulled out my .38 and jumped out of the aircraft. Were any enemy lurking about?

In a few minutes a Huey came to our rescue and picked us up. Our company commander had been returning from a mission at Lane Army Heliport and had heard my emergency call and position. Whew! The AC pilot and I never talked about that episode until 50 years later at a reunion. *Our versions differed somewhat.*

After a couple of months as a slick pilot, I had made AC and was flying regular missions, I became disillusioned with the way things were going. Why didn't we just march up Highway One, the road connecting Saigon and Hanoi and go into Hanoi and get this thing over with? We had the necessary fire power but seemed to lack the will. Politics seemed to say that if we used excessive force then Russia and China would join in and nuclear war would ensue.

We were sitting ducks, grouping in our LZ's and bases. The NVA/VC always knew where we were. We never knew where they were. They fought when they wanted to. We reacted to their initiatives. Our major thrusts were always known to them. They had spies at all levels from the hootch maid to top officials in the Saigon briefing rooms. We had no spies. They had Jane Fonda. What the hell was she doing on their side? I suspected foul play and wondered about General and President Eisenhower's warning, *"Beware the military-industrial complex"*.

My head was awash with ideas. My fighting spirit had long ago abandoned me as I searched for meaning and justification for this situation. I contemplated flying to Thailand with my helicopter. I could open up a brothel and live happily ever after. Too far away by helicopter. Maybe I could fain insanity and be taken off flying status. I could fake it, but would I be able to find my way back to reality, when I wanted to?

So I approached my company commander, a Major and another Kansas man from Council Grove who had recently been infused into the company. Company commanders only had to serve 6 months and then they too would change positions. Who thought up this merry-go-round of replacements?

"Sir, after due deliberation, I'd like to transfer to Dust Off and be a medivac pilot. I think I'm more philosophically inclined to be involved with rescue operations and serving the wounded," I announced.

"Well, son," said the Major, "You've been trained to be a combat officer. Our gunship platoon leader just got killed and the assistant gunship platoon leader went down with him.' I want you to be the new gunship platoon leader." I gulped. "You think about that for a day or two," he said.

Chief Zogleman said, "Sure, you can be in the 'guns'. Everybody wants to be in the 'guns'. You get to shoot back! We'll break you in and show you the ropes."

I somewhat reluctantly agreed. Hey I'd always liked hunting and guns, but this was different. Then I remembered those night missions of the slicks. Landing in a dark, foreboding, tree-shrouded, small, make-shift LZ on a pitch-dark, moonless, overcast, foggy night had never appealed to me. Gunships provided the covering fire. That sounded like a better job. Later I found out that 40% of Dust-Off Medevac missions were at night, just the kind of missions that I dreaded.

My tenure as 3rd platoon gunship leader resulted in several memorable occasions. Daily or weekly, as the occasions arose and assaults were planned, we covered the missions assigned. The warrant officers, great pilots, the crew chiefs and technical inspectors, and especially one E-6 sergeant who came to my rescue, all knew what to do. I let the best most qualified members be involved in the planning and execution of maintenance, rearming, and daily affairs of platoon management. I meanwhile also had extra duties. I had various reports to complete such as safety reports on downed aircraft and Officer Efficiency Reports, and was charged with obtaining lumber and materials to build all the rest of the company proper Vietnam style hootches and get our guys out of tents.

A former enlisted man, now an experienced warrant officer and the E-6 sergeant were most helpful in this regard. Through back channels, bargaining and the good will of a neighboring engineering detachment, we got the necessary materials. The men eagerly pitched in to build the structures and the task was completed in weeks.

One dark night, we were called out to support troops that were being fired on by machine gun fire coming from a village. We saw a couple of rounds coming out of a straw structure and directed our fire that way. I was just learning to fire the weapons and got no response when I tried to fire a rocket. "Recycle your circuit breakers," said team lead Starblazer 13, Chief Zogleman. I did as suggested, came around and punched off a rocket. Whoosh, went the entire volley of 14 rockets! The helicopter seemed to stand still in midair as the force of the rockets exiting their pods pushed back. The outside lit up like a searchlight. The rockets completely demolished the hut. No return fire was received. Well, I should either be awarded a medal for single handedly neutralizing an enemy position, or did I kill innocent civilians whose hut had been invaded by hostile forces and using them as a shield had fired on the Americans. *I'm not sure about that.*

Chapter 6. A Seasoned Veteran Now.

And then there was the time, much later when I was more experienced, a platoon was being attacked by a superior force of NVA. The Americans had their backs to a river and in front of them was forest, a small clearing, a tree line and low brush through which the bad guys were slowly creeping up and attacking.

"Put a rocket between us and them', said the RTO, ground radio operator. I did and the next time around he asked for a round a little closer to him as the bad guys were still creeping up. "A little closer to us, next time," he said again. Just as I was punching off another rocket a gust of wind jostled the aircraft, swinging the nose to the right, my foot slipped off the right pedal and I thought, Oh my God I'm firing a rocket into our guys! I was as scared and perplexed as I'd ever been. Long seconds intervened until I heard the RTO's next call. "That's close enough! That's close enough!" The enemy withdrew and faded into the forest. As I surveyed the area, I noticed a beautiful water fall in the background. *Wonderful place for a picnic.*

I never counted the days while I was in Vietnam. I remembered the maxim, "A watched pot, never boils." So I just went from day to day knowing that someday my time would be up and I'd be able return home to experience real life and some semblance of sanity.

I did get to go on R&R, Rest and Relaxation, and take a one week leave while in Vietnam. I went to Japan, met some nice people, and to Australia. In Japan I encountered an American in a restaurant who was seemingly aghast at my presence in the dining establishment. As I walked past him, he pulled back from brushing against my sleeve as though I had a contagious disease. I was surprised at his reaction but later figured that this was an anti-war protestor's response. Australia was more fun. A fraternity brother friend who was in the Air Force had called me on Christmas Day of 1968 and we planned our R&R in Sydney. I was duty officer that day. The rest of the company had gone to Phu Cat Air Force Base to see Bob Hope and Raquel Welch or some equally voluptuous maiden. This was when I was new in the unit so I had the lowest seniority of any RLO and somebody had to do it. Fortunately, I was right in the Operations shack, a low-lying sand bagged bunker, when the field telephone rang and through the crackling on the wire I could hear my college fraternity brother, now a Lieutenant in the Air Force stationed in Saigon, say, "I want to speak to Lt. Embers." "Hey Bob, it's me," I replied. We made plans to meet in Sydney with one month left in our tours. I figured that I could go on R&R and fool around long enough so that when I got back, I could start preparing to exit the country.

We had a good time in Australia. In fact I decided that after I got out of the service I would return to Australia and take up residence. It was so quiet and peaceful. The attitude of the people was so hearty and robust, they loved to drink beer and there were many beautiful young women. One day Bob and I needed to withdraw money from our bank accounts in the U.S. so we went to an Australian bank. They told us to go upstairs and we arrived at a spacious room filled with gorgeous female bank clerks. Bob and I thought we were in Heaven. But, I never went back. I went to France instead.

After returning from Australia, I found the unit had moved from LZ English back to Lane Army Airfield where our maintenance was stationed. We now had a rustic stone officers' club with a bar, and sometimes exotic dancers would perform, well once. Missing were the sultry Asian beauties that I had envisioned and Veronica Lake. We had showers, concrete floors and a little PX. There was a small church there too, but I never went inside. This was really living, but I was ready to get back to the States.

However, there was one last big mission that we were going on. The new company commander, a West Point graduate, called me in, gave me my captain's bars and informed me that I was in charge of setting up the refueling operations in the highlands for this major action that the Americans and Koreans were going to launch. Wow, already a captain. *Rank came easy during combat. Just stay alive.*

"Who's going to supply us with the equipment," I asked. "That's what you need to determine, keep me informed," said the CO.

I had no idea where to turn for help, so once again I relied on my former enlisted man warrant officer and the E-6 sergeant. Eventually we made arrangements through the engineering battalion in Quy Nhon. Our company commander reluctantly pitched in to finalize the operation. Was this some kind of a test? I only had a week to go before I was scheduled to go home. Usually one didn't fly the last couple of weeks, but not this time.

We flew high up into the neighboring mountain range. Actually, it was only a couple of thousand feet, but coming from sea level it seemed quite different. We hauled troops for several days, moved them all around chasing the NVA/VC wherever we could find them. But they never showed up. They knew we were coming. They had spies everywhere and they knew that we were supporting the ROK's, the Republic of Korea, Army. The enemy wanted nothing to do with the Koreans. The Koreans were terrors in their own right. Whenever we inserted Koreans, they went to every village and hut, searched it and burned it down. Their policy was that anybody who lived in an area not controlled by the friendlies was in enemy territory and the inhabitants were ipso facto the enemy. The Koreans didn't make any friends. I loved working with them because wherever we took them, there was usually little to no enemy resistance.

Chapter 7. Home Free

I shaved off my combat aviator's mustache, and left Vietnam aboard a TWA airliner with a cheering group of veterans and landed in Seattle, Washington, at the SEATAC airfield. Snowcapped Mt. Rainier was in the window as we landed. I hopped off and transplanted a kiss from my lips to the sacred Mother earth of America. I was home. The sympathetic magic technique of visualizing a desired outcome had worked. I had planned for this day. I was lucky.

In the restroom, as they called the latrines stateside, all the enlisted men were shedding their uniforms and throwing them in the trash. I was wearing my favorite short sleeve khaki Army uniform and don't think I had any civvies to change into even if I had wanted to, which I didn't.

I ordered up a bloody Mary on the way from Seattle to Wichita and relaxed in the last row of the airplane. The drink reminded me of Vietnam and all that I had left behind. It sure was good to be back. At the airport in Wichita a huge crowd awaited me and a ticker tape parade, flowers and garlands were strewn along the path with beautiful girls to sit alongside me as we cruised along main street. I was given the key to the city, a Cadillac and ticket to go anywhere I wanted with whomever I might choose. All I wanted to do was go home.

Actually, only Mom and Dad were there to greet me. It was good to see them but felt strange. I sat in the back seat on the drive back. I still had two years to do at Ft. Rucker. My Dad suggested that I make a career of the Army. "After all, you're already a captain and you haven't been in 3 years". It was true, a career in the Army would offer financial security and opportunity for advancement. But I didn't want that and I certainly didn't want to go back to Vietnam. One tour as a helicopter pilot was enough for me. Later in 1986 as I was looking for a job, I remembered that if I had stayed in the Army I would be retiring after 20 years, if I had lived that long. I couldn't imagine being in the Army if there was no war going on either.

My San Francisco girl, the one that I wrote occasionally and had kept me company on those long dreary nights in Vietnam wasn't available when I returned. She had met another, but I appreciated her past contribution to the American fighting force and my personal well-being. Then I met a really nice girl when I got back. A hometown girl that exemplified all that I had been missing. She was beautiful, soft and warm, clean and nice and had greenish brown, hazel eyes. She too made life worth living, though our time together was short. During that time, I inadvertently displayed a crudeness or drunkenness that offended her and we ended our brief affair. *I had changed.*

I had another job to do before I was through with the Army, or they were through with me. I was going to be an instructor pilot at Ft. Rucker, the Home of

Army Aviation. You get to say where you'd like to be assigned when you return from Vietnam, or at least you get three choices on where you'd like to be assigned. I had picked the Army's Safety School at the Presidio in California as my first choice. If not that, then Psychological Operations at Ft. Huachuca in Arizona in the Intelligence section would be a good fit, and lastly Ft. Belvoir in Washington. D.C. to fly VIP's around. I was assigned to become an IP, Instructor Pilot, at Ft. Rucker.

Oh well, now I could really learn to fly. I wanted to be an instrument instructor pilot. This would allow me to get a standard instrument ticket and further my flying career opportunities. And so I did. It was kind of a letdown to go back to flying OH-13's, the Army's instrument training helicopter at the time, but it was OK for a while. Then I became the Fort's airspace officer, in charge of all the training air space at the fort, the beacons, navigational aids and maps. We simulated the location of towns and cities in Vietnam to accustom pilots to their future AO, Area of Operations.

I knew something was wrong with me when I woke up one morning after a drinking spree at the Lakeside Officers Club on post. I had managed to drive home and stagger to bed but in between something unusual had happened. In the middle of my small BOQ apartment was a pile of splinters and broken pieces of furniture. I had completely smashed to smithereens a nice captain's chair that went with the dining table. I was filled with rage at something. *It scared me*.

Then I met Sue. She saved my life. The time flew by after I met one of the most charming southern belles in L.A., Lower Alabama. At least she made life bearable and enriching for the two years of our acquaintance. She taught second grade and her family had a farm nearby. We went dancing, swimming in the Gulf of Mexico, attended functions at the Officers club. I was one lucky guy.

But I had other aspirations. I wanted to travel internationally. I discovered that I could get the G.I. Education Bill if I attended approved universities in other countries. I had incurred a three-year obligation to serve in the Army by going to flight school. I had spent one year in Vietnam and two as an instructor pilot and air space officer. So, when my time was up, I decided to leave the Army and live abroad.

I wanted to go to the University of Grenoble in France. I bought the cheapest ticket possible on Iceland Airways and stopped in Reykjavik, Iceland, on my way to Lyon, France. I had always wanted to go to Iceland. They heated their homes with steam from volcanoes, imagine that. I chose Lyon because it sounded like a friendly place, after all my home town was near Lyons, KS. Everybody went to Paris so I wouldn't be going there. I wanted a small-town atmosphere.

Chapter 8. France

Lyon, France, population 6 million, was where I attended an intensive French language school. I needed to bone up on my college French to attend the University of Grenoble. I couldn't speak French hardly at all even though I had taken several semesters in college.

I stayed in the language school dormitory but it was expensive. I was on a budget now though I had saved a considerable sum while in the Army. In fact, I paid off my school loans and saved thousands of dollars while drawing captains pay, flight pay, combat pay. I bought a brand-new 1970 red Volkswagen Beetle with a sun roof, then sold it when I left the States two years later. I imagined a future of traveling around Europe and the world. Maybe hiking and staying in hostels. I had some time to make up. The Army had been a diversion and I had some living to do.

Then I met Pat. One day I went to the Bank of America in Lyon to open up an account. Mr. Janvier, the bank vice-president, took a special interest in me when he found that I had been a combat helicopter pilot in Vietnam.

"I've got a friend that's got a job for you in Africa," he said.

Well, I didn't want a job as a mercenary and I didn't want to go to a politically disrupted country in Africa. I wanted to learn another language and live in another culture, sure. My sociology degree had spurred my interest in other people, places, and things, but not in a war zone. I had tried that in Vietnam and war totally disrupted the experience. I wanted to try out France first, learn French and learn about the culture of some of my European ancestors. Besides, I had just arrived, was in school and my future was just around the corner.

Disappointed, Mr. Janvier motioned me to go to the cashier's counter and open up an account. He said, "Go on over to that young lady cashier. *She will take care of you.*"

I was pleasantly surprised to be cordially greeted by a saucy, fresh, clean-looking young woman who efficiently and matter of factly made all the arrangements for me to open an account. We chatted pleasantly as I wondered which French guy was dating this really nice American girl. She spoke French, German and of course English, being from Ohio. She had blond ginger-colored hair fashionably pulled back around her neck in a perky pompadour, blue eyes, and wore a blue dress.

I struggled with learning French through the total immersion audio-visual approach. I don't recommend it at all, maybe as a punishment for masochists. This method makes you guess the answer. Who needs that when you could be told the answer in your native language? This method could be used as a supplement or a change of pace, but it's really not efficacious or efficient.

Because of my difficulty with learning French, I became interested in how was the best way to learn a language. My plan had been to go to France, meet a nice girl, a French girl, and really learn how to speak French. I still think that's a good way, but it wasn't to be my way.

The best way, by the way, is to study the grammar, read books with conversation in them, and watch videos with subtitles in the language you want to learn. This is to learn how to speak and converse in another language. That's the fun part. It's so amazing to utter phrases in another language and have the person respond accordingly. Like wow, I'm making these sounds and they understand me. This is great! Reading is easiest, then writing, listening and speaking, in that order. A bi-lingual friend is a big help.

I walked all over Lyon, then I bought a Gitane Gypsy racing bicycle with 12 gears. I roamed all over, started living in a Catholic monastery with a Japanese friend I'd met and eating meals with a bunch of monks. It was free, or I was free-loading I guess you'd say, but there were restrictions. The place closed down, locked the gates and doors in the early evening. Sundown was bedtime, but not for me. Coming back late I had to scale the 10-foot wall around the perimeter of the church and monastery, then sneak in through a basement door which was left unlocked. Then feel your way through the large wine cellar, wine at every meal, and grope your way up to my room.

I wanted to buy a van so that I could spend the summer going to Sweden's off-coast island of Gottland to visit some of my ancestors' graves and relation on my Grandmother Esther Eleanor Eklund Embers' side. I had in mind a VW bus, and sure enough one day as I went back to the Bank of America where I had an account, a white VW van, for sale, was outside the bank. I went to the bank to check on my account and to check on that nice teller who had waited on me when I opened my account.

I bought the van, although it was a little newer and more expensive than what I was looking for. I had to transfer money from my stateside bank account to my French account, so Pat, the bank teller from Ohio, probably thought I had a lot of money. I kid her about this, but she denies any connection.

I went to a French-English club one night with an American friend. The Americans that I met in France were the most interesting folks, they all had the urge to travel like me, and were open to adventure. A bevy of girls walked by and I spotted the bank teller. Hmmm, I approached her and we struck up a conversation that has lasted over 50 years and is still going on.

The van increased my mobility, range and number of friends. We went hiking, spent overnights visiting villages and towns, roamed the countryside, clambered up some mountain trails, and let the wind blow through our hair. Every weekend was an adventure. Marseille, Barcelona, Geneva, Monaco. These would be long 3-day weekends, but who cares, whee!

I converted the VW Kombi van to a camper by taking out the back seats, putting in a hinged bed and place to make coffee and cook, sort of, on a little gas burner. We lived the carefree life of American expatriates enjoying France, Spain, Germany, Holland, Denmark, Norway, Sweden, Switzerland, Europe and the Mediterranean.

But all good things come to an end they say, and Pat returned to the US of A. She had planned to return before I arrived and had continued her stay in France to be with me. Realizing that I wasn't the marrying type, she disputes that, and that she had other fish to fry, she hopped a train out of Lyon and then flew back to Ohio to visit her folks before journeying to Boston where she started her new life as an occupational therapist.

I meanwhile had come to realize that after one year and nine months in France, the excitement and newness had worn off. It was the summer of 1973, the oil crisis was on, wheat prices were up to $5 a bushel and my Grandad

Embers needed help on the farm cutting wheat. So I bought a backpack, put all my things in it and headed for Paris in my VW van. There I sold it to the new American consulate who was an acquaintance of a friend of mine and caught a plane from Paris to New York and then to Kansas City. I hitch-hiked on home and presented myself at the front door of my parent's home in McPherson, KS.

Chapter 9.   Second Homecoming

"Oh my God," said Mom. "What have they done to you?" she wondered.

I had lost about 30 pounds from eating irregular meals, walking a lot, bicycling, and running carefree through life. I hadn't shaved or had a haircut since I had gotten out of the army in 1971. And it was 1973. My jeans were patched, I had a back pack, a sun tan and I smoked Gauloises cigarettes, the iconic cigarette of the common working man in France.

We headed out to the farm to help with harvest. Grandad Embers was hurrying from the garage workshop to the barn in search of parts for the combine. I greeted him with a big bear hug. We had never hugged before but I was so glad to see him. He reeled back in surprise, and looked at me quizzically. Was this his grandson? What the heck had happened to him?

I jumped up on the combine, when we got it running and started cutting wheat. It felt great to be in the open air, listening to the roar of the combine, watching the header bar and reel gobble up the golden heads of wheat.

Just before we had finished cutting the last field of wheat the combine broke down and was irreparable, at least without a major overhaul, so I suggested that we call my other grandfather, Grandad Bird who had finished his harvesting and was doing custom cutting. It was great to be working with both of my grandfathers out in the wheat fields. This was to be their last harvests as both were in their eighties and due to retire.

My Grandad Embers asked me at the end of the harvest, "Well, what do think about taking over the farm?" I was shocked; in all our years of working together he had always told me not to go into farming, but to find another field of endeavor more promising than farming. He had actually wanted to be a school teacher. He was a smart guy and so after he had finished the eighth grade, the local school board suggested that he go to eighth grade again, and that this would qualify him to become the school teacher the next year. This he did, and for several years he taught school. He wanted to go on with his education and become a certified teacher, but he was one of 4 boys and a girl in a family that couldn't afford to send him off to a teacher's college. Grandfather was also frustrated that some of the students, who were a lot older than he, since they didn't go to school regularly, had not earned the requirements to graduate. They would not follow his instructions and would just get up and leave the classroom on their own cognizance. Very frustrating to a teacher. Also, the pay wasn't much. So when he got the opportunity, he decided to get married to one of his beautiful Swedish students and start farming on the home place. Now here he was asking me if I wanted to go into farming.

I had endured several summers during high school and college of farm work. I found it to be boring, hot and uninspiring though I like the outdoors. I wanted to go back to college, get a master's degree in linguistics and language education, so I respectfully turned him down. He agreed that it would be a difficult task to take over the farm as he had planned everything out so that when the equipment, the combine, tractors, trucks, etc. wore out, he would be worn out himself. So that was the last harvest, but it was also the most financially lucrative for him and many other farmers at that time.

I then entered graduate school at Kansas State University. I almost got an MA, but decided that I was smart enough and didn't do a master's thesis. This was, of course, a mistake that I regretted in the coming years. But it all worked out, because instead of getting involved in the upper echelons of administration of my future jobs, I worked more closely with students and was able to develop programs more attuned to their needs, or at least that's what I tell myself.

Pat and I corresponded and she came to Manhattan, KS, to visit; then I suggested that she come back and stay, which she did. We moved to an old converted school house in the country where I got into raising honeybees at the suggestion of long-time friend Bob Kelly. We then bought a small house with a little barn in Olsburg, KS. I converted the barn into a honey extracting shop with concrete floor, hot water, 30 frame radial extractor, grew to a hundred bee hives, and started the Blue Valley Honey Co.

Then encouraged by Lin Rose, another friend, became a Vista Volunteer and first president of the Downtown Manhattan Farmers Market in 1979. I worked at the Adult Learning Center in Manhattan part time teaching ESL, English as a Second Language, and Pat worked as an O.T., Occupational Therapist, in several small-town nursing homes. In 1977 we had taken a trip to California for Pat to attend an O.T. workshop, and decided to get married in Zephyr Cove, Nevada, on Lake Tahoe. In Olsburg we lived life fully and comfortably in a "back to the earth" style, burning wood to keep warm, growing our own food and living simply. Our family developed as we had a daughter and a son who unfortunately passed away at one and half years of age. Our daughter Sheila, is the pride of our lives and has just bought a home in Portland, Oregon. My father always contended that our bad luck in having kids, several miscarriages, and of course our son Christopher's death was a result of my exposure to Agent Orange in Vietnam.

I had been heavily exposed to Agent Orange. We sprayed Agent Orange in the An Lao Valley over the mountain range to our west. A slick would fly low level over the trees and jungle foliage spraying the herbicide while the gunships would cover them, in case they got shot at, took enemy fire. The mist flew all around us and we thought nothing of it. We were just clearing away some brush so that we could better detect enemy movement.

In fact, we were polluting the river that ran through the middle of the valley. It was a nice river, but it had become muddy and dirty due to run off from the adjoining hillsides. The ridgelines had been bombed and blasted with artillery thus denuding them and allowing the harsh monsoon rains to wash the soil into the river. When I went back in 2010, the trees had all grown back and lush verdant foliage covered the hills and valleys preventing soil erosion. The rivers had recovered, at least that one had, and it was clear and navigated by boats and ferries. The fishing was good, too.

During the Vietnam War, the U.S. Air Force dropped motion sensors up and down the valley to detect enemy troop movement. An Air Force officer came to us one day wanting to go out into the valley and check on the placement of these sensors. We took one slick and landed in an area that had a trail passing through it. I jumped out armed with my trusty .38 revolver and noticed a cultivated area hidden back under some trees. There was a well-tended garden there and a reed basket of hot peppers setting on the ground. It suddenly came to me that I was being watched. What the heck was I doing out here by myself? I grabbed the basket and hurried back to the helicopter. I still have that nicely woven basket. What did I know? What an idiot. Someone was living there, in spite of all the military activity.

I started working part time at the American Institute of Baking, in Manhattan, where we later moved, teaching baker's math and ESL. Teaching math was an interesting and educational learning experience for me. I had started out at KSU in mechanical engineering, then I switched to chemical engineering for the 2nd year, so I had had math all the way up to Calculus 4, differential equations, etc. When I got to engineering physics and quantitative and qualitative analysis in chemistry, I decided to switch to a major that was more interesting. I wasn't too good in math but loved the concepts in chemistry and physics.

I learned that the best teachers are not the best students, au contraire, the best teachers are former students who struggled with learning. This allows them to identify learning hurdles and explain subjects clearly and in depth with lots of practice problems to insure complete mastery of the operations.

I had to teach "Baker's Math." No problem, until I started doing the ratio and proportion problems necessary to figure out the amount of each ingredient needed to make a certain batch size or pounds of dough. I couldn't do the problems, even though I had been exposed to advanced math. The solution was that bakers use a special kind of formula percent called "baker's percent". *Some genius baker* discovered that if you let the weight of flour equal 100%, then you could express all the other ingredient proportions in relation to the weight of flour. For example, a simple bread formula or recipe may call for 100 lbs. of flour, 60 lbs. of water, 2 lbs. of yeast and 2 lbs. of salt. By expressing the ratio of ingredients in a percentage format, one could make any size batch you wanted, 10 lbs. of dough, or 150, or 2000 or any amount. Bakers always use weight measurements because volume measurements e.g., teaspoon, cup, gallon varied by ingredient. A volume of water weighed more than the same volume of flour. Using Baker's Percent meant that the total formula (recipe) percent would, in this case, be 164 %, not 100%. If it was too salty, just drop the percent of salt, say to 1.5 % of the total flour weight. All the other ingredient percentages stayed the same. Remarkably convenient when adjusting for taste, consistency and handling characteristics. *Genius baker who understood basic math.*

I also learned the value of the metric system, which is based on 10's. Every unit of measure, volume, weight and length in the metric system is a multiple of 10. Changing from meters to kilometers is simply a matter of moving the decimal point to the left three places, in other words dividing by 1000. In our customary system, the inch-pound system, it's necessary to remember arbitrary standards such as "one mile equals 5,280 feet, or 1760 yards, or 1 lb. equals 16 ounces, or a foot equals 12 inches, or a gallon equals 4 quarts, etc. This extra step in converting units causes undue consternation to our children in grade schools and discourages the appreciation of mathematical concepts.

National Metric Day is October 10, 10/10 of every year; the tenth day of the tenth month. The metric system is a scientific system of measurement used by the medical profession, engineers, scientists, the military and now mechanics in every country.

It would be wise for the U.S. to adopt the metric system and make unit conversions more straightforward. As I mentioned, in our current measurement system, which is called by various names, e.g., (British, standard, common, customary) converting inches to feet requires dividing by 12, and converting ounces to pounds, dividing by 16. In the metric system it only requires moving the decimal point or dividing or multiplying by multiples of ten to convert centimeters to meters and grams to kilograms. That's only one example.

Here's another: In the metric system, 1 gram of water occupies a space of 1 cubic centimeter which is the same as one milliliter. That means that there is a direct conversion from a weight unit to a volume unit of measurement. We don't have that in our inch-pound (customary) system. One ounce of water does not occupy a volume of one cubic inch. For example, 1000 grams (weight) occupies 1000 milliliters (volume) or one liter. You know what a liter bottle of soda is, it's just a little larger than a quart. But a quart contains 57.75 cubic inches of water. See how confusing this gets when using our current system of measurement?

Converting between the two systems is also confusing because it requires memorizing conversion factors, much like using our current system. It's much more efficacious, efficient and fun to just use the Metric system of measurement. We already use the decimal system with money, e.g., 1 dollar equals 100 pennies or cents.

We can all appreciate that the basic concepts of physics and chemistry are really interesting and useful, but using the customary cumbersome inch-pound system, inhibits our children from being the best they could be. Besides, and I add this humorously, we could drive 120 (kph) on the Interstate highway, and I'd only weigh 72 (kilograms).

Then there is the matter of fractions, ½,¼,1/5, and so on. It came to me that 6th grade math concepts are about all you need in life, unless you plan a career in science or engineering.

Note that 1 over 2, or ½ means one divided by two, not two into one as you often hear people say. There is no "into" key on a calculator, only a "divide by" key. One half equals .5 when done on a calculator. And that decimal amount, .50 is equal to 50% when changed to a percent. If you know how to convert fractions to decimals and to a percent, and know your multiplication tables up to 10, you can "estimate" answers. All or most all successful people use "estimating" when making personal or business decisions. For example, if I invest or buy $5,000 worth of stocks or bonds and the return is 10%, then I'll make $500 per year off that investment.

But if you missed class the day that the teacher explained how to divide fractions, i.e., invert and multiply, then you are forever one of the "I don't like math cause I'm not very good at it" types. I find math useful, especially when flying helicopters or airplanes, or driving a car or doing the bills at the end of the month, or estimating how far my social security check will go.

Algebra is useful too. It's the next step up in abstract thinking. Abstract thinking is the ability to derive concepts from what we observe physically. Recognizing patterns, analyzing ideas, synthesizing information, solving problems, and creating things all involve abstract thinking. That and the ability to speak an abstract language is what separates humans from animals. Of course, some other animals can do it, Roy Rogers' horse Trigger, Lassie, the Wonder Dog, and Francis the Talking Mule come to mind. Modern day equivalents, well, you would have to ask a younger person. Artificial Intelligence, AI is based on abstract reasoning and experiential repetition. Who knows where that will lead.

In 1969, when the U.S. sent men to the moon, I looked up at the moon one night in Vietnam and thought, "Now if we are smart enough to send a person to the moon, why aren't we smart enough to figure out how to resolve conflicts without blowing each other up and killing each other?" Or at least, if that's just human nature and we are going to keep doing it ad infinitum, why haven't we invented helicopters that don't need a pilot and we just steer them around from a remote position? *Once again I was ahead of my time.* We have that now and also the ability to home in on some poor unsuspecting dude and wipe him off the face of the earth. OK, maybe he's a bad guy to us, but it seems really grotesque to go on international TV and crow about killing someone. What kind of example is that for our children; a revenge mentality? I think there is a primitive religion based on that. Surely, we need an increase in human mental emotional quotient or EQ. Our IQ or Intelligence Quotient exceeds our EQ, emotional quotient. We are great at figuring things out like nuclear power and the atomic bomb, but not so good at human relationships. That could end in us using our technical knowledge to blow ourselves up and self-destruct. However, since some corporations and the military industrial complex thrive on war, a nuclear holocaust that wiped out almost everybody would not be good for business; no customers. So, no need to worry about that unless a politician or megalomaniac has access to this power. Hmmm.

Algebra was named after an Arab guy, Al Jabara, or something like that, who realized that you could write down a simple mnemonic device to help you figure out some interesting things. For example, the area of a room in your house is found by multiplying the width times the length, Area = length x width, A = 20 ft. x 20 ft, Area = 400 square feet. If it's a triangle then Area equals ½ base times height, or A=1/2 bh, and if it's a circle or you have a center pivot irrigation system or an impulse sprinkler for your yard, then it's Area equals "pi" times the radius squared. Oops, now we are moving into more interesting abstract thinking. What's "pi"? That's just the ratio of the circumference of a circle to its diameter, you know, the distance around a circle in relation to the distance across a circle, 3.1416. Radius is the distance from the center to the circumference.

Anyway, you can go a long way using this kind of thinking. Einstein used this algebraic notation to express his famous theory of relativity, E=mc2, Energy equals mass times the velocity of light times itself or squared. The velocity or speed of light is 671 million miles per hour, mph, so if you take some mass, say an atom, and speed it up to around 450 quadrillion mph, it bursts into E, energy. I guess that's how they make atom bombs, but don't quote me on that. I've reached my abstract thinking limit, I think.

FYI, quadrillion is the number that comes after trillion, which means it's even greater than the U.S. national debt of trillions of dollars. When we start talking about spending quadrillions of dollars, that'll be some real money, albeit, inflated dollars.

One day the president of AIB, American Institute of Baking, Dr. Bill Hoover, where I was working part time, called me into his office and asked if I'd like to accept the position of Director of Admissions. This was a huge opportunity for me and a challenge. I said OK, but he said, "Not so fast, this is a big job and a responsible, full-time position. You need to discuss this with your wife and think about it. I told Pat about the offer and she was delighted that we would now have a steady paycheck and health care. She just said, "Well if that's what you want to do, then I think it's a good idea." Wasn't she great. I returned to his office in a week and agreed to accept the position. I assented because our son Christopher had serious health concerns and as our family developed, we did need health insurance and a steady paycheck. We had some big hospital bills to pay and AIB graciously consolidated and covered them, to our immense relief. My greatest fear was once again that I would be confined to an office and not be able to roam freely as I was wont to do.

It was really hilarious that I had been offered the job just as I was telling the story of my initial Vietnam "scramble team" experience to Ralph and Scott, a couple of the maintenance engineering instructors at AIB. I had just gotten to the point where one of the seasoned veterans had asked me if they could have my electric fan, in case I didn't come back from the midnight scramble mission. We were sitting in my office drinking coffee and I was smoking a cigarette, at that time you could smoke inside, a nasty practice, and over the building intercom boomed the message, "Ken Embers, report to the President's office." What, me to the pres's office? I didn't even know he knew me. Well, we had met in the restroom one day; he had asked who I was and I informed him that I taught ESL, English as a Second Language, and math part time and drove the van to pick up the international students for ESL class in the evening. He and I were just zipping up having used the urinals. I offered my hand in greeting and we shook, so I reckon we became some kind of brothers, *not exactly blood brothers but we had a special bond.*

Earlier, in response to the request for me to report to the president's office, I put out my cigarette, took my feet off my desk, straightened my gig line, and hitched up my pants. As I was leaving, one of the maintenance instructors said, "Can I have your fan if you don't come back?" One of them was a Vietnam vet and the other a Korean war vet, so that style of humor was easily understood. *There is something about being with combat veterans that is satisfying.* I guess you identify with being scared out of your mind, or having performed some gloriously heroic action. Actually, it's between that, you just did what you were trained to do and used your own good sense, hopefully.

The students at the Institute were usually full-time employees of major baking companies in the United States and abroad. Many were from Japan, Mexico, China and the Philippines, some from other countries in South and Central America, Europe, and other Asian, African and Middle Eastern countries. The international students, due to their lack of English proficiency, especially required attention, so I assumed the mantel of International Student Advisor along with being math and ESL instructor, financial aid director, housing director, scholarship chairman, tour guide extraordinaire, director of AIB correspondence courses and admissions, and the audio-visual director. This was a fascinating job, and I had the freedom to attend any of AIB's many one-week seminars to learn about baking, food production, and food safety. I also got to travel to many foreign countries representing the AIB.

The American Institute of Baking was a unique organization. It had been established in 1919 to address the growing need for expertise in the field of large-scale production of baked products. Louis Pasteur, back in the 1860s, along with a cure for rabies and the "pasteurization" process had discovered the scientific basis of the fermentation process. He had been hired by the wine makers in France to address the problem of wine turning to vinegar. He proved that living cells, yeast, was responsible for two types of fermentation, aerobic, with air, and anaerobic, without air. As a result of his studies, commercial production of yeast was made possible. The Fleischmann brothers came from Austria-Hungary, partnered with an American businessman and built a yeast plant in Cincinnati, OH. This meant that the baker no longer had to rely on bacterial and wild yeast fermentation to make bread rise. In other words, you didn't need to make bread from a sourdough starter or by using the foam off of brewing beer. Commercial yeast raised bread revolutionized the bread-making industry making it possible to provide tons of bread for the American soldier "dough boys" of WWI.

The Institute was an internationally recognized source of information and education for the baking industry. Most major baking companies all over the world sent their employees to the AIB for training. We offered correspondence courses, one-week seminars, a four-month intensive course for production supervisors, maintenance engineers, and special seminars for researchers, food labeling analysts, food safety auditors and inspectors.

In addition to serving the needs of the commercial wholesale baking industry, world renowned artisan bakers gave special seminars on the techniques of making gourmet products like sourdough bread, French bread, boules, baguettes, Danish pastry, cakes, cookies and crackers. The "art" and craftsmanship of artisan baking, combined with the "science" of baking taught by AIB was a powerful combination. Whole grain and multi-grain products became popular as nutrition and the public's taste for artisan style products grew. The industry had changed since before WWI when homemade bread or bread made in a local bakery was popular and available. The invention of the band saw type bread slicer and introduction of Wonder Bread in Missouri in the '30s saw a revolution that led to the phrase, "greatest thing since sliced bread".   Then the military determined in WWII that many draftees were undernourished or lacked vitamins, so the baking industry attempted to rectify that by "fortifying" or enriching white flour with B vitamins and nutrients. "Builds strong bodies 12 ways" was the slogan. People had preferred white flour products since ancient times when royalty got the white bread, the starchy endosperm of the grain, while the peasants got the left-over wheat germ and less refined flour. Come to find out, the vitamins are in bran and wheat germ. In an attempt to satisfy both the desire for white flour products and to make white bread more nutritious, B vitamins and other nutrients were reintroduced into the white flour. You could have your cake and eat it too was the goal. If one could make a baked product that was both appealing, light and fluffy, tasted good and was good for you, eureka! Whole grain products tended to have a somewhat bitter taste from hard red winter wheat, the primary flour used in bread-making, so more sugar or honey was added. Then honey became too expensive and another discovery of how to turn corn starch into fructose or liquid sugar through enzymatic activity, led to using corn sugar and high fructose corn syrup in baked products. And if you still didn't like the taste of whole grain cakes and cookies, just cover them with chocolate icing. Fascinating stuff, and the search goes on.

The science of baking explained the function of all the ingredients in bakery food production beginning with basic science. This includes ingredients and processes, such as, salt, NaCl, water, H2O, chemical reactions between an acid, vinegar and a base yield salt and water, the different types of yeast, sugar, shortenings, oils, lipids, flour grades, nutritional content, the fermentation process, bacterial fermentation vs. yeast fermentation, caramelization, and the browning process called the Maillard reaction. Lots of great stuff that turned math haters and people allergic to or afraid of chemistry into aspiring science buffs when they realized that *the world around them was one big chemistry experiment.*

Not only did the AIB do research on modern production processes and introduce them through their educational programs, it provided sanitation information and guidelines for the baking industry. As the food industry grew after WWI, cleanliness and improved working conditions for the employees became of paramount importance.

Some of the larger baking companies asked AIB to help them with local, county, state, USDA and FDA food inspections. The AIB Sanitation Department grew from an auxiliary service to the baking industry to providing food safety good manufacturing practices to other and large segments of the food industry. Eventually the department, AIB International's Food Safety Department, exerted an international impact on food production. The high standards and integrity of the staff exceeded government requirements and came to be considered a kind of "insurance" policy for food production companies. If you could pass an AIB Food Safety inspection, there was no doubt that you would pass a government inspection.

AIB Food Safety audits were eventually adopted by the largest baking company in Japan when they had a problem dealing with the cleanliness of some of their incoming ingredients, flour in this case. Through the AIB Education department, the company was introduced to AIB food safety standards. The vice-president of food safety, Bill Pursley, a practical, insightful, experienced, former food safety auditor, convinced the visiting team of top echelon executives from the company that AIB could "help you solve your problem". This one phrase was much different from the advice they had received from several other private food safety companies that they had sought advice from. Those companies all tried to "do the job for them", rather than "helping them solve their problem". This practical approach was a key element in the department's success.

As the Food Safety department grew in stature and revenue, the emphasis on "profit centers" within the

AIB increased. Originally AIB was started as a service to the baking industry, and was supported by donations and participation in programs that provided needed information and training. This was done at a cost-effective price that provided the companies with a reasonable return on investment, an investment in research and education.

In the '70s and '80s, state sponsored colleges and universities changed from being "public" universities to becoming "private" universities. The major portion of funding no longer came from the state which provided low-cost tuition for residents, but shifted to private and federal grant funding. Grant funding meant that research scientists worked to achieve a specific purpose that benefited the grantor, but was not independent basic or advanced research. Tuition rose astronomically and more research funds were provided by private corporations "who", not "which", since corporations are now legally regarded as persons, *greatly influenced the direction of research and education*. Recognizing corporations as "artificial persons", according to Supreme Court Justice William H. Rehnquist, and according to Pres. Barack Obama in a State of the Union address, has "opened the flood gates for special interests, including foreign corporations to spend without limit in our elections". Not a good thing. We need to re-visit the interpretation of the 14th Amendment which originally aimed at guaranteeing all the rights of citizenship to formerly enslaved people.

AIB followed this pattern and **devolved** into a private food safety pest management company.

Seeing that income from food safety programs was making a profit for AIB, the IRS determined that the sanitation inspections were indeed a private profit-making business. A shift in AIB administration started to marginalize the "service" nature of the baking school and research department programs and accentuate the profit-making arm of AIB.

Good business practice you might say, or as one AIB vice-president characterized it, "The tail started wagging the dog". The AIB Museum of Baking, the best accumulated history of the commercial baking industry in existence, and the library, were all dispersed to various parties, private individuals and locations. The museum included baked items found in the pyramids of Egypt. Baked bread and beer were found to be staples for the workers building the pyramids. The builders of the pyramids weren't slaves, they were seasonal laborers who were paid and served some of the world's first and finest processed foods, baked bread and beer.

The price of educational programs at AIB rapidly increased and expensive travel to the Manhattan, KS, location for instruction and training was replaced by technological improvements and delivery systems. On-line courses became standardized and replicable and the personal interaction waned. AIB started taking the educational programs to the customers through seminars and in-plant training, but this proved to be not cost-effective for the Institute. More pressure was put on the Education and Research departments to be profit-making centers, which they were never designed to be.

Improvements and advances plus financial support in these areas declined. "All good things come to an end," someone said.

Chapter 10.   Library of Vietnam Project

One day in 2010, Mike Meyer walked into my office. He represented the Kansas Agricultural Hall of Fame and wanted to partner with AIB. Even more importantly, when he saw a replica of a Huey helicopter on the credenza in my office, he mentioned that he had been a door gunner on a helicopter in Vietnam.   From there we went to talking about Vietnam and what had happened there since our time in the war. He worked with several veterans' programs and mentioned one in particular, the Library of Vietnam Project, started by Chuck Teusch, a Vietnam veteran.

I contacted Chuck and expressed an interest in his project of building libraries in Vietnam. About the same time Chief Zogleman, Mike, called me with an offer to return to Vietnam on standby tickets. I agreed and a couple months later we joined Chuck on a large speed boat ride up the Mekong River to Phnom Penh, Cambodia to visit a library he had started there.

Phnom Penh was amazing and enlightening. An occasional elephant still walked down the street bearing trade goods. The gold leafed pagodas' roofs and newly renovated government buildings shone brightly as citizens practiced tai chi exercises while the sun rose over the Mekong River and music wafted over the entire spectacle. We visited the infamous "Killing Fields" where Pol Pot had murdered thousands of Cambodian citizens for being intellectuals and wrong thinkers who opposed his dictatorial communist ideas of re-establishing a mythical Khmer kingdom based on a self-sustainable agrarian society. His goal was to make Cambodia great again by cutting off contact with all foreign influences and curtailing the destructive influences of western culture. Maybe not such a bad idea, but his methods were so despicable.

In the early part of his campaign to control Cambodia, both China and North Vietnam supported him. After a series of government flip flops involving Sihanouk and Nixon's bombing of rural areas, Pol Pot's government became insufferable to the recently victorious North Vietnamese who invaded and overthrew Pol Pot's regime. Here I apologize for over simplification and lack of details and understanding. Another senseless violent attempt to garner power and achieve something, what, a utopia? *"Never happen G.I."* This phrase was often used by the Vietnamese to express the non-likely hood of an event occurrence, such as buying a product or service at a reduced price.

We visited the LOVP library near the Killing Fields. Kids were provided with a small two-story building that housed books, magazines and instructional materials. There was a black board, tables and chairs and an area for study and teaching. Upstairs in a small kitchen area food was prepared and we enjoyed a simple meal, some of the food coming from a garden and fruit trees on the grounds.

From there, Chief Zogleman, Larry Cooperrider and I went to Bong Son, Vietnam. Bong Son was the little village beside LZ English where I had been stationed for the most part of my one-year tour in Vietnam, '68-'69. Larry was the best man at one of Zog's weddings, I had been the best man at another one of his weddings at Ft. Rucker, another of his weddings he didn't count as it had never been consummated or was of such short duration or something to that effect. Larry had been drafted right after graduating from high school.

Larry was point man for a unit of the 25th Mechanized Infantry Division. They had APC's, Armored Personnel Carriers, and their mission was to provide security for the main thorough fares and highways and roads used by the local citizenry, the ARVN and US troops. Usually this was a two-lane black top road built by the French years ago. They also went on sweep missions designed to dislodge the enemy from the terrain surrounding the roads and bridges necessary to move men and material when and where necessary. The U.S. Army and the ARVN wanted to drive out the VC/NVA so that Republic of South Vietnam could be established as a free and democratic country. The VC/NVA were seeking to establish a communist unified country which included South Vietnam.

Larry was a farm boy. He went right into the Army out of high school and was in Vietnam after only four or five months training. Basic Combat Training, Advanced Individual Training in the infantry at Ft. Benning and there he was in Vietnam. He had a level head, was smart and alert and not afraid of anything. He carried an M-79 grenade launcher and on his hip he had a .45 automatic pistol. He was "point man," the guy who led the platoon through the bush and into unknown territory. Somebody had to be first and Larry was that somebody. He did that for about one year and was never wounded nor blown up. But the drama of being point man was intense as this was serious life and death business. At the end of the year, after having been shipped around Vietnam, but never really knowing where he was or what he was doing in relation to the "Big Picture," he was returned home to his farm in Ohio, near Columbus.

As we navigated the countryside of Vietnam by bus, boat, train and car, Chief Zog, aka Mike and I talked about all the places we had flown to and why and Larry began to put together where he had been in Vietnam and when and why. This return to Vietnam with comrades in arms and especially helicopter pilots who supplied details of larger troop movements during their time brought together a kind of elucidation for Larry. It cleared up some things in his head.

"You know I was drafted, trained, sent to Vietnam, did my tour and spit back out in the course of less than two years", he explained. "When I got back to the States and hopped back in my street rod and started cruising the streets, it was like I just woke up from a dream. Did that really happen? I've been going to PTSD group counselling sessions regularly ever since that time. I've been married, now divorced, raised two fine young men who help me, rather I'm helping them now. I farm, and have a great girlfriend. I'm a successful agri-businessman and farmer, but I never understood what that was all about until I went back to Vietnam. I'm good with that now."

Lots of veterans go back now. They remember and honor their friends in combat and come to terms with the longest most impactful year of their lives. Some don't want to go back, of course. The memories are too painful. "I didn't leave anything there," they contend. "What, you're going back to help the effing gooks?" is another comment.

I wanted to see what we could find out about LZ English and establish a relationship with the Vietnamese people by building a learning center in Bong Son. A library learning center where kids and adults could come together and read, do research, learn English and talk with American kids and adults through the emerging technology of computers, smart phones, FaceBook, video chat and Zoom. Most of those things hadn't been developed yet but they were soon to come about.

We approached the local school authorities with the idea of building a library. We said that we would supply the blue prints, the plans, and money to buy the materials and hire the workers to build the 61st Assault Helicopter Company Library Learning Center. "Really?" they replied questioningly. They were astounded that anybody from the USA would even think of them or of proposing such an outlandish venture. "OK, sure, yes", was their answer, "But", and I paraphrase, "this is a communist country and you don't start doing things at the local level, you have to get permission from the government in Hanoi and that has to work down through the province headquarters in Quy Nhon through the Department of Foreign Affairs, and then to us."

"OK", we said, we'll do that".

Chuck Theusch, founder of the Library of Vietnam Project, now known as "Childrens Library International" had already established the LOVP as a duly registered NGO, non-governmental organization, with the government of the Socialist Republic of Vietnam in Hanoi. He had already built several libraries and was keen to offer his aid in helping us build a library learning center in Bong Son.

He made the administrative arrangements, got all the papers stamped and met with the head of the Dept. of Foreign Affairs in Quy Nhon to get the final OK. "Are you guys for real?" was Mr. Tan's comment. This had never been done in the history of the world. A combat helicopter company coming back to a region where they had been actively engaged in trying to repulse an opposing force and a way of life that now controlled, administered and lived in the area, to build a library learning center.

What was the rational for all of this? "If you can't beat them, join them," some might say. I didn't think in those terms and I didn't think that this was some sort of "guilt" resolution trip. I thought that establishing a communication network with the people we had formerly been at war with was a good thing to do. *War is an old fashioned, counterproductive, out dated, obsolete, archaic form of conflict resolution and we can do better than that.* Let's get some communication going and see what happens. I learned to appreciate international people and cultures through my college studies in sociology, living in France, visiting other countries as a working professional, and as a kid, National Geographic Magazine was a great introduction to appreciating the way people lived all over the globe.

Once we started this project, we developed relationships. During the almost two years it took to build the Library Learning Center we made several trips to oversee the process and check on the progress. I was amazed to see that the hard work of constructing the two story, 40 ft x 60 ft building was mainly done by women. The bamboo ladders and scaffolding were all erected by women, the concrete blocks were hauled up the scaffolding by pulley, and so was the cement masonry. Men mixed the mud or cement and the general overseer was a man. The School District Supervisor, was a well-educated, no-nonsense woman who made sure that all financial transactions were transparent and out in the open. We presented them with fresh crisp $100 bills, over 400 of them.

Recruiting donors for the project was one of the most satisfying things that I've ever done. About half of the guys in the 61st Assault Helicopter Company who had been in Vietnam one time or another were interested in financially participating. Spouses, girlfriends, former girlfriends, school teachers, moms, dads, brothers, sisters, other Vietnam vets and interested parties all chipped in to provide the funds.

During the dedication ceremony in 2011, Pat and our interpreter sang a song of friendship in Vietnamese. Pat, who had received a music scholarship to attend Ohio State, played the oboe, and had taken opera singing lessons in Germany, spent several/many hours listening to the song and learning the Vietnamese pronunciation. They loved it! Then some of the children serenaded us with several songs, one in English. They were very professional and very loud.

Chief Zog, Mike, presented some paintings done by a Vietnam vet to hang in the library and I gave a short talk about how our purpose was to provide a place for their individual and personal edification, especially for learning English, and to establish a communication network with them.

We always ended our visits with a dinner at a local restaurant. On one occasion, fried crickets were offered as a special delicacy. Most of us ate them, quickly washing them down with Heineken beer. Heineken was now the beer of choice. Originally a Dutch beer, it was made in Vietnam now. They also had Tiger beer and Ba Ba Ba beer. When we were there during the war, Ba Muoi Ba beer was common. Ba muoi ba means 33. Now the Vietnamese have the new improved variety Ba Ba Ba beer, which reads 333. An obvious upgrade.

I've been back every year since, except for during the Covid-19 lock down in 2020-22. One year I spent six weeks teaching ESL at a vocational trade school in Phu My near Vung Tau. My main students were young Vietnamese men who wanted to emigrate to Australia and work as welders.

There was a demand for welders in the oil field industry around Perth and surrounding areas, and a Vietnamese community was developing there. The Australian government required a certain level of English fluency for an immigrant to receive a work visa. All the students were highly motivated to learn English and pleased to have an American teacher that was familiar with safety procedures and understood the terminology of construction and the industrial work force. Thanks to my involvement with the AIB's food safety and occupational safety programs, I could familiarize them with the terminology required to pass certain entrance requirement tests to gain employment. The Vietnamese guys wanted the relatively good paying jobs that were available in Australia, and in return would send money home to support their families.

Vietnamese children learn from an early age that they have a duty and an obligation to their parents and ancestors to take care of the family and support the elders of the family. Veneration of past generations as the originators of the current generation is a sacred duty. Personal gratification is achieved by being a good provider, while a person that neglects their family is seen as a derelict aberration that will suffer ostracization and misfortune in the future. *The selfish person is not a good person*. This admirable trait of filial piety governs much of the family interaction that somewhat replaces religion for the Vietnamese.

Although Vietnamese culture, heavily influenced by 1000 years of Chinese domination, is oriented towards the Confucian values of order, respect and hierarchy in the family, to teachers, to the local government officials, state authorities, and the national government, most Vietnamese claim to have no particular religious orientation. There are Buddhists and Catholics and several other religions such as Cao Dai, an interesting combination of Buddhism, Christianity, Taoism, Confucianism and western philosophical persons and ideas. There is the traditional Vietnamese folk religion which honors life in all its forms, but there is no strong belief in a main God like Christianity promotes. *No heaven, no hell.* Just do your best for you and your family, especially your family.

Consequently the U.S. idea of saving the Vietnamese from the atheistic communists who contended that "Religion is the opiate of the masses," seems to have been a misguided effort to project a Christian mind set upon a society and culture that could care less. Ngo Dinh Diem, the president of South Vietnam, was a Catholic and this "authorized" him and gave him a stamp of validity in the eyes of the U.S. political and military administration that accelerated our involvement in Vietnam's civil war. Eighty-five per cent of the Vietnamese claim to have no religion, or as one Vietnamese interpreter lady friend said to me when I asked what religion she was; "I'm nothing, I'm free"! Four percent are Christians, mainly Catholics, 2% Buddhists, some Cao Dais, Islamists, and others. There is a Confucian mentality of respect, order and hierarchy in cultural and societal affairs. The Vietnamese have a strong tradition of honoring their ancestors and famous people who contributed to society. *It's believed that the spirit of the ancestors is still a viable influence if honored and respected.*

The current government of Vietnam promoted a visionary program of encouraging all Vietnamese citizens, including kids, to learn English by the year 2020. Now, everyone in Vietnam has the chance to learn English. Kids start in 3rd grade and study English 45 minutes a day, 3 days a week at least. There is a thriving industry of private classes and schools that give English lessons after school and on weekends.

Why would the Vietnamese want to learn the language of their former enemy? As we know, it's the world language of business and scientific exploration. Everybody speaks English now, or at least some form of it. Well not everybody, but those engaged in the international affairs of business and education certainly do. And if they don't, their kids do or are learning.

Chapter 11.   Globish

A subset of English, called Globish, pronounced with a long "o," as in "globe", is spoken by more people than any other language in the world, whether they know it or not. More people speak Globish, a form of English, as their second language in China than there are native speakers of English in the United States. It's not an all-encompassing, slang-filled American or British English. but it is English that is quite effective for international commerce.

Globish is a discovery and codification of a concept developed by Jean Paul Nerriere, a former IBM vice president of marketing from France . Nerriere noticed that as a non-native, i.e., English as a second language speaker, he could communicate adequately with Japanese or other businessmen for business purposes. But when an American, British, Australian, Canadian or other native English speaker joined in the conversation, that communication was hindered by the rapid pace of vocalization and the use of non-standard phraseology. In other words, native speakers spoke too fast and used idioms like "Howdy, how you all doin', what's up, etc."

Nerriere and David Hon, an American entrepreneur, Vietnam veteran Marine Corps officer, ESL teacher, sailor, developer of the world's first realistic medical simulators, artist and author, wrote the book, *Globish the World Over,* to explain the concept and encourage use of the insights that derive from this way of thinking. If native English speakers would learn and use Globish, it would facilitate communication around the world. Plus, it would generate a respect for the difficulty of learning another language well enough to express your thoughts.

A native English speaker needs to learn to use direct sentences in the active, not passive voice, using only the 1500 most common words in English and their derivatives, while speaking somewhat slowly and clearly. An example would be to say, "I like ice cream," in the active voice, versus, "Ice cream is liked by me," using the passive voice. Words common to a topic or profession need to be added of course, but these are easily learned and familiar to speakers interested in the same subject. Combinations of those 1500 words can yield a vocabulary of 4,000 words, which is an average speaking lexicon for a native speaker. Although there are about 200,000 words in English, new ones coming along all the time, and we recognize 80,000 more or less. Most people only use about 6,000 words when speaking, some lots more and some a lot less, of course. So you see, learning 1500 words will enable a second language learner to carry on an intelligible conversation and do business, discuss topics of interest, and resolve differences if any should arise, *depending on the emotional quotient of the individual.*

One of our Vietnam veterans, Sgt. Major Ross Worley, Special Operations Forces, Green Berets, retired, of Kansas City, has semi-adopted, encouraged and financially assisted a Vietnamese girl since she was in college majoring in English. Now she has become an in-demand ESL teacher in Phu My, Vietnam. Thuy, English name Joel, works for the public school system and offers extra classes in class rooms in her home. She develops fluency in spoken English in her students by involving them in dynamic role-playing and gamesmanship in a fast-paced competitive environment that keeps the kids enthusiastic and excited to learn. This is not easy and is a special talent that she has learned over several years. It helps that she is a dynamic extrovert that senses the inhibitions and blocks to learning inherent in language learning. She is able to project her enthusiasm to her students and involve them in activities that develop not only their fluency but their thinking on logical and moral issues. There are no shrinking violets in Joel's classes, or if there are, they soon bloom.

There is a joke about language learning that is only funny to international students. It goes like this: Do you know what they call a person who speaks 3 languages? Answer: Tri-lingual. Do you know what they call a person who speaks two languages? Answer: Bi-lingual. Do you know what they call a person who speaks only one language? Answer: American. Ha ha, probably you didn't think much of that insight but it's true. Only 1% of Americans develop fluency in another language despite having taken a foreign language somewhere in their schooling. It's difficult to learn to speak and communicate in a second language, but billions of people are learning enough English to survive and prosper in today's global economy.

When one travels, the residents of a country always appreciate it if you can speak their language, or at least try. It's important to try to learn how to pronounce names and places just so you can get around more easily. You also learn how difficult it is for someone to make the unusual sounds necessary to properly say someone's name.

The story could end here, but this is not the end. There are lots of great things in store for the children of Vietnam and America and the relationships that develop out of our interactions. Perhaps in the future, there will be fewer thoughtless, violent conflicts. I guess that wouldn't preclude violent conflict with a purpose, usually in defense of family and homeland, but a lot can be accomplished by learning a common language.

In this next chapter, we'll look at what has developed since our time in Vietnam and some of the ramifications and considerations that evolved from that experience.

Chapter 12.   Life After a Death-defying Experience

A common myth is that Vietnam veterans are druggies, slackers, the homeless and disgruntled ne're-do-wells. While it is true that many veterans feel used and would give you cautionary advice about meddling in other nations affairs, it's not true that most veterans are derelicts. My research has shown that most veterans were above average Joe's that survived and became fairly, but not fully, well-adjusted American citizens with a good work ethic that resulted in being fairly prosperous tax-paying citizens. Some, most, even grew stronger from this experience. *Adversity develops character.*

Here are some short bios of some of the guys in my unit. I asked how they got into flying and/or what they did after Vietnam. They agreed to sending me this info for inclusion in this essay. I won't use any names, so they can't sue me in case I misquote them if I mis paraphrase their responses. Well on second thought, to give credit where credit is due, I've decided to use the names they provided.

This first one is one of the longest but is an example of a Vietnam vet "gone good". "What an interesting memory ride to take", it starts out.

Bernie Busby:
Did my obligatory college and drop-out cycle which netted me employment with IBM Federal servicing

office products on site. A suit and tie netted me clearance into the Joint Chief's of Staff war room and additional stints at Atomic Energy Commission. All at age of 18. My IBM career really didn't suit me and having been seen by the Draft Board 5 times in 8 months (registration, student deferment, drop student deferment, occupational Defense Dept. deferment, drop occupational deferment), I sensed induction was on the horizon.

Speaking with my US Army Recruiter and asking for a job in automatic data processing (now IT), I told him of having a few lessons in an Alon Ercoupe in my mid-teens. He queried me about me being interested in flying helicopters. I jumped on that; however I wasn't quite ready to sign. I did some partying until I received a letter from the draft board. I called the recruiter and told him I was ready to sign up that day. The next day I called and told him I had a letter from the draft board. He wasn't too happy since it meant he had to do more paper work to clear my draft.

Survived BCT (basic combat training) at Ft. Polk and with 2 weeks delay en route, met up with friends back home in Maryland and one of them was high school acquaintance of the female persuasion and started a successful letter writing campaign. (More about that, later.)

Pre-flight RW (rotary wing, helicopters) at Wolters brought an offer to go directly to FW (fixed wing, airplanes) initial entry at Rucker. I along with my pre-flight brothers resisted, insisting we had contracts! I got my way and moved on to 3rd WOC

(Warrant Officer Candidate), Blue hats, with one class 4 weeks ahead and one class 2 weeks behind. (The war was pretty busy in 1967!)

The timing of flight school worked out so we got 2 weeks Christmas leave, returned to Wolters for 2 weeks in January, then 2 more weeks delay en route to Hunter AAF. It was during this time that I speed dated my relationship with Gina and by February I was engaged to be married! Scheduled end of flight school - June 4, '68. Scheduled Wedding date – June 8, '68.

During the beginning of tactical phase, my brother-in-law died and I took an emergency leave to attend the funeral. I was counseled it might result in me being recycled and add two weeks to my graduation date. I made the round trip to Norfolk for the funeral and back at Ft. Stewart Tuesday night. I guess my standing was pretty good, no recycle.

At graduation, I was ordered to Ft. Eustis for Aircraft Maintenance Officers' Course which gave me a 4-month honeymoon in Williamsburg, VA, before deployment! And some Wednesday night flying in OH-13's and T-41's.

Turning 20 on October 4, I deployed on October 20 to RVN (Republic of Vietnam). Assigned to the 17th Group saw my first casualty; another tenant of transient BOQ placed his bunk directly under the ceiling fan and during the H and I fire (harassment and interdiction), he sat bolt upright into the metal bladed fan. Pretty bad injury. I believe he was sent home.

Processed through the 268th BN at Phu Hiep and on to Quy Nhon. Lt. Rod Orndorff gave me a jeep ride on to Lane Army Heliport for a short 1 day in-process. Then on to LZ English to be my home for the next 8 months.

Marv Papka was one very happy WO (warrant officer) when I arrived. Marv had been given the extra (read that all the time) duty as forward maintenance officer at English. Marv's desire was to go the Starblazer gunship platoon and after giving me a month OJT (on the job training) he was on his way. The 'Blazer shack was next door to the maintenance shack. (Marv also tried to teach me some guitar chords, e.g., "He was a Friend of Mine". Took me a looong time (20 years) to eventually play decently!)

This 20-year-old learned a lot very quickly. Since I had picked up the duty, I made it a point to get with Lt, then CPT Duane Briggs, 61st Ops Officer, to fly as often as I could with superior pilots. Kyle, Pennington, Vieux, Zogleman, and many others. I particularly recall learning from John P. McDaniels how to use the tools you have. I had great night vision and took a liking to instrument flying, so John and I would do flare missions – JM: "You fly, I'll talk." (John dreamed of going to the 1st CAV and I believe eventually got his wish!)

In addition to improving flying skills, Jim Hogeboom taught me how to mess with grunts. Jim always spit shined his boots and when we arrived at firebases or outposts, the troops would bust on him about hootch maids and shined boots. He never let on that we didn't have such amenities.

After return from R&R in later June, I was relocated to Lane to work directly with CPT Jim Moulton (an AMOC classmate) and CPT Rod Landorf, CO of the 616th TC Co, our direct support at Lane. Many more night test flights and GCA's (ground-controlled radar approach) into Phu Cat (Air Force base). Turned 21 and 2 weeks later DEROS'd to Hunter AAF where I wanted to teach instruments (flying with no visual reference, night, bad weather). I was assigned D Co, 2nd Maint Bn, at Evans AHP, Ft. Stewart. Lot's of rotating shift work to support the Flight School tactical training. It was there I scored a shortfall into a POI class and qualified as a UH-1 B,C,D and H instructor.

Back-to-back family misfortunes in Spring '70 afforded me a compassionate reassignment to Ft. Meade, MD, where I found a unit with 135 "absentee pilots", many enrolled full-time at local colleges. "We have no room for another pilot." "Oh, OK, I thought you could use a Huey IP." What!! Absolutely, step right up, and I joined the Air Cav Troop, 6th ACR, designed to defend the region.

Soon qualified as UH-1 SIP and obtained my Standard Instrument rating and was assigned to fly the CG (commanding general) First US Army, (no competition with the VIP crews at Davison AAF). When 6th ACR moved to Ft. Hood, I moved over to the First Army Flight Detachment. LTG Hutchin loaned me to ADM Noel Gayler, Director, National Security Agency and NSA trips and missions began.

Late 1971 on to Rucker for instrument examiners course, and January '72, AH-1G transition enroute back to RVN. Got to fly Cobras against tanks during the siege of Kontum. When the 361st Panthers shut down, moved over to the 57th Gladiators, as unit SIP and IFE. Wound up January 1, 1973 at Team 21 flying BG John Kingston under the peace treaty. Left RVN March 28, 1973, and left the Army.

Past favors for the Reserves while on duty at Ft. Meade resulted in finding a slot with the 327th (later 196th) Avn Company. Drills and man-days helped me fund my University of Maryland studies while supporting my bride and two daughters.

CH-47 qualification in July '74 broadened my horizons and in September, '75, started as a DAC with the USAR flight facility in Hagerstown, MD. Part-time work flying BO-105 and AS-365 for local coal company. Three years later moved to Willow Grove NAS as a DAC and assigned to the 453rd ASA detachment. Signal intelligence for the next 10 years as a Reservist.

Joined FAA District Office in Teterboro, NJ for a year and half when my fortunes brought me back to the Washington, DC area with assignment to the US Deparment of Energy as aviation safety program manager. Nuclear criticality training at Las Alamos, Occupational and Environmental Radiation Protection at Harvard School of Public Health. Working with both Defense Programs (now National Nuclear Security Administration) and the power marketing administrations kept me traveling throughout the US spending quite a bit of time developing flight safety programs for business and paramilitary activities.

Finally led back to the FAA, this time on the Flight Standards staff in Washington, allowed me a type rating in the BE-350 and Citation 550. I got to finish out a government career while proficiency flying out of Hangar 6, Washington Reagan Airport.

After retirement, the phone gradually started ringing for consultation support. A little flight instruction in light sport aircraft and a five-year stint as a charter boat captain in the summers filled some of my time. Closed the logbook with just over 7200 hours flight time. Fifteen years spent auditing airlines under the IOSA program; repossessing bankrupt airline aircraft; auditing Naval vertical replenishment operations, multiple trips to the Middle East and Africa, and visiting 6 continents in 2 years at the end of the line. Fifty-two years celebrating flight school graduation and our wedding in the same week. And very thankful to have been in touch with so many of my aviation friends over the years.
Merry Christmas and a very Happy 2021!

My what a story eh? One time, "and this ain't no bull shit either" (most aviator stories start out this way), we were flying home in a Huey gunship to LZ English and the hydraulics went out. We could barely control the helicopter as the cyclic and collective were stiff and barely responsive except with a lot of pressure, and stuck when moved. In a helicopter you need a light touch to control the many micro movements necessary to make a helicopter perform normally. We also didn't have good tail rotor response so the helicopter wanted to turn in the opposite direction in which the rotor blade was turning. So, we kept up our airspeed to streamline the aircraft and get the nose pointed in the right direction and skidded to a landing on the short runway, just the way we were trained to do in flight school. Whew, we made it. Cheated death again. Called maintenance, and said Maintenance Officer, Bernie, came over. He berated us for landing over on the landing strip, jumped in the helicopter and flew it over to his maintenance facility, somehow managing to fly that onery critter and land it on a dime. Quite a pilot!

Now Chief Zogleman, after whom this narrative is partially named, has quite a story. But like many adventurous daredevils, he doesn't say much except when armed with a beer and a funny smelling cigarette. Here's his response to my query:

Mike Zogleman:
Went to college out of high school, dropped out and joined the Army. In Vietnam 1968-69 and extended 18 months. Next tour 1971-72 flying Chinooks (big two rotor heavy lift helicopters). Instructor at Ft. Rucker upon return. Married there. Was at Fort Riley and then to Alaska with the Army. Got out after being in Army seven years. Answered an ad in Trade

The Amazing Adventures of Capt. Embers and Chief Zogleman

a Plane to fly physicians in Ohio. Then started an aviation business (PPS – Professional Pilot Service). Then flew for Jiffy Lube as their Chief Pilot. Divorced and married Kathy, current wife. After Jiffy Lube did odd jobs, but then moved to Iowa to fly for a for-profit juvenile delinquent facility. Lost that job via Dany Pennington (fellow 61st pilot who offered a better job). Went to Guam and flew Saudi Arabian princes and other missions. Two months on and one month off. Bought a farm in Iowa - still farming. 5 kids, 8 grandkids, 18-20 moves since Nam.

Chief Zogleman added this story too: "My mother wrote me in 1969, said my cousin was in Vietnam, I should look him up. Right Mom, 500,000 soldiers here. Within the next couple of days, I was resupplying some grunts in the Sui Cao valley, looked out and saw my cousin in front of the helicopter. I yelled at him; he thought I was screwing with him and gave me the finger; go figure. He was a grunt in the 173RD Airborne. On future lifts I would hear on the intercom, 'it's your cousin, said he would not get on until I picked him up.' This sure played hell in single ship LZs. Later, I took him to the Lane officer's club, dressed him up in civilian clothes, said he was Captain Montgomery. Great days!"

What the Chief leaves out is an epic story in itself. He bought an airplane in high school, instead of a car, getting an early start in the flying game. His dad managed a small airport in El Dorado, KS. The Chief was the Standardization Instructor Pilot for the 61st AHC in Vietnam, having demonstrated outstanding proficiency and good air sense. He was young and unafraid as many 22-year-old WO's were, immortal and loved flying in Vietnam. After the Army, for a while he was a bush pilot in Alaska, a fixed-wing instructor pilot, a Life Flight helicopter pilot ferrying patients from crash site to hospital, and a test pilot for Beech Aircraft in Salina, KS, for several years. He had many Harley motorcycles, hot cars, several wives and a few accidents which eventually slowed him down a bit. And also, some farming incidents, like when his tractor ran over him and his sons saved his life by calling 911 and getting him to a hospital, ironically by helicopter. He was a natural pilot and never had an aircraft accident, but with other machinery and vehicles, not so lucky. He once said, "I'm kind of one dimensional, all I can do is fly aircraft." Not exactly true, as he was also a good farmer and cattle rancher, rode and showed horses with his kids in 4-H, a good gardener and a friend. Now, a regular mass-attending Catholic, he has a Beechcraft 35 V-tail Bonanza, the sports car of private aviators, a 2005 red Mustang convertible, has traded in his former Harley Davidson Road Glide Special for a new HD Trike Try Glide Ultra, and he spends time on his country estate in Iowa, swimming in his pool with grand kids, singing in his personal hot sauna with his big "Starblazer" tattoo on his right upper arm, and listening to outlaw country music. I'm not sure about the singing part.

More pilot stories:

Dave Quimby:
Enlisted in the Army in helicopter flight program. Took direct commission and did two tours in Nam. Was in the Army 8-9 years. Taught Primary helicopter flight training for 26 years at Ft. Rucker until retirement. Was in Nam 1968-69 and 1971-72. Married for 48 years, 3 kids, 6 grandkids, 1 great grandkid, in the Army 20 years. 15-18 moves since Nam.

Ed Luck:
In 1964 went from high school to college. Had to attend night school to get grades up but draft was heavy, so in 1967 a recruiter said they needed helicopter pilots. Had never flown a plane but joined up. Crashed in Nam. Attended first VA meeting 1993. After Army drove trucks from 1976-84. Then started a job in a paper mill. Married in 1980, went back to college and graduated in 1989. 2 kids, 5 grand kids, 2-3 moves, retired in October 2008, in the Army for 3 ½ years.

The fact that Ed's last name was Luck was appropriate. I once asked him to fly the Huey that took me and the Air Force officer on our recon mission to check on the status of "motion detector" devices that had been air dropped out in the An Lao valley, as I've mentioned earlier. Many years later at a reunion, Ed remarked to me. "You know we were crazy to go and land out there in the An Lao Valley with no gunship cover." He was right, we should have had gunship cover. Luck, Ed.

Jeff Lines:

Out of high school wanted to fly as dad was in the guard. Enlisted. Went to Nam-flew first mission with Marv. Extended – went through TET 1968. Went back to the States and was a first lieutenant. Was with the air defense artillery branch. Made captain. Went to Iowa and got fixed wing, multi-engine license. Went to Lafayette and flew helicopters – would resupply oil rigs in the Gulf of Mexico. Flew lots of different places with the same company. Left in 2007. Married, divorced but married now. Have 1 daughter, no grandkids. Active in the church. Working on a business venture. Was in Nam 1968-69, 8 moves. Was in the Army 5 years and 3 months.

I learned an important lesson from Jeff. One morning we were returning from Lane, our maintenance support and HQ, on the way to LZ English with the mail. It started raining with a tremendous cross wind force like nothing I'd ever seen in Kansas. I was a brand-new FNG (fricking new guy) and it was the monsoon season. We couldn't see, couldn't maintain visual reference, so Jeff dropped down to a couple hundred feet above ground to maintain VFR, "visual flight rules", also ironically called IFR, "I follow roads". Actually, IFR means "instrument flight rules." Still we couldn't maintain contact with Highway 1 and couldn't see ahead, so Jeff made a 180, turned around, as he commented, "We could attempt to fly through this localized shower, but we're not sure it gets better up ahead. We could go left or right and look for better weather, but we do know one thing, where we came from the visibility was better, so here we go back where we came from. There was the possibility that the weather had closed in behind us and we were SOL, shit out of luck, but fortunately it hadn't. So we peeled back, found an opening, ascended and flew out towards the South China sea and around the weather. This is an example of making a good decision. Often an attempt to "tough it on out" when flying is not a good decision. Just "trying harder" and "hoping for the best" in a helicopter doesn't necessarily lead to success. Sound decisions based on experience and logic works better. There is the pilot's saying, *"There are old pilots and there are bold pilots, but there aren't a lot of old, bold pilots."*

Marv Strawn:

Was in the ROTC and went to Ft. Riley for summer camp. Loved flying as a kid. Was in the ROTC flight program. Got a fixed wing license. Went to flight school and went to Nam in a boat with the 61st AHC as a newly formed unit. Was in Plei Ku and waited for helicopters to arrive. Unit became operational in 1967. Left the army. Got into a truck company. Went to law school. Practiced in Madison, WI. Was in the US Attorney's office. Went back into the national guard. Worked for a pipeline company for 2 years. Hired on at Alice Chalmers. Worked in a bank for 14 years. Then worked in a small law firm. Retired now. Married twice – once for 20 years and then 25 years. 3 kids (5 including wife's kids), 8 grandkids, 4 moves. Was in Army/Guard for just under 30 years. Was in Nam 1967-68.

Marv was a level- headed experienced captain and I only got to fly with him one day. He rotated back to the States in a couple of weeks, so I never got to learn enough from him. This was the problem with being a replacement. You didn't get to know the lessons learned from the previous pilots, those that survived. We hadn't instituted a formal unit or company history informational program. It wasn't a part of the SOP, "standard operating procedures". We should have had briefings from those experienced pilots before they left. They could have summarized what they learned and passed it on to the "newbies".

Marv wrote a more extensive summary of his time in Vietnam for his children. I'll include it here, when I find it. OK, found it, here it is:

Marvin Strawn:
Flying & post-Vietnam life: I know I was less than 5 years old when the flying seed was planted because my first airplane ride came while our family lived with my grandmother from 1945-1949 in a very small town near Rockford, Illinois. My father's brother at that time owned a small plane with a friend. One day my uncle flew to the town where we lived and landed in a farmer's hay field just south of town to give us rides. I remember clearly sitting on my dad's lap watching the world grow smaller as we took off and made our short flight. I remember being silent and interested, not at all restless from start to finish.

In 1965, between my junior and senior year of college, I went to Ft Riley, KS, near Ken Ember's home for my six-week ROTC summer camp – a sort of boot camp for ROTC guys. During the various orientation briefings, someone asked if any of us were interested in flying. We had to have 20-20 vision, most parts of our body, and weigh less than two hundred pounds. If we signed up now, we would also get free private flying lessons during our senior year in college. I signed on the spot without discussing it with anyone in or out of my family. I got the private license the Army promised me in Ames, IA, and, of course I still remember soloing. After takeoff, I laughed out loud and talked to myself in a jolly voice. My conversation with myself that day was basically: "You stupid jerk, you got yourself up here but how in the Hell are you going to get down!" But I wasn't worried about landing, I was loving the experience!

Flight school was not much different for me than anyone else who loved flying except, in one respect. At Ft. Wolters the WOCs were flying the Mattel Messerschmitt, the TH-55, while commissioned officers were learning on the old Hiller OH-23s. One day I and two other second lieutenants were notified that from then on we would do the flying part of our training with WOCs in the TH-55. The story was that the Army wanted to see if it would be difficult for students to transition from the very forgiving Hiller to the much more responsive Hughes. The story seemed like BS to me. I always thought they needed some Hillers to teach some higher-ranking officers to fly, but I didn't care. I just wanted to fly. As a plus, the WOCs were fun on the bus rides and I liked the difference between TH-55 and Hiller which was something similar to the difference between a sports car and a family sedan.

When I entered the Army, I thought I might make it a career, but even before Vietnam I had serious doubts about whether the Army and I were compatible. I liked the flying a lot but often found the Army annoying. I flew slicks in Vietnam, got around 1100 combat hours in ten months of flying, had all the usual experiences of slick pilots. I absolutely loved the freedom of flying in Vietnam. Unless you were flying formation, the pilot decided how the helicopter would be flown, what it could do and what it could not do. I came back to the "land of the big PX" about November 1, 1968 feeling very positive about the flying part of the experience. But I also came back even more convinced the Army and I were not meant for each other. Several months of teaching Tactics at Ft. Stewart, GA, probably helped cement that feeling since I did not enjoy the school flying nearly as much as the flying in Vietnam, and maybe actually disliked it.

In August, 1969, I left the Army to go to law school at the University of Wisconsin. I still wanted to fly and there was a Guard helicopter unit right in Madison. I called the unit and totally misunderstood how much flight time I would need to get monthly and felt I would not be able to put in that much time and go to law school. Instead, I got a truck company to help pay for law school. I also checked with a private helicopter flying service nearby, but when the owner said he didn't like former Army pilots, I bid him a quick goodbye. For various reasons, I left the Guard on graduation from law school and did not get back in for four years. By that time, I had not flown in seven years, had in my mind reverted to amateur status as a pilot, and, for that reason, did not try to fly with the Guard.

On graduation from law school, I was a Wisconsin Assistant Attorney General in Madison for three years prosecuting bid rigging and price fixing. Our antitrust group was successful enough that we recovered from the bid riggers more than three times our total budget. We were a profit center for the State, almost certainly the only profit center in Wisconsin government. After three years I moved to the US Attorney's office in Madison to join the guy that hired me at the Attorney General's office. There I did both civil and criminal trial work. When Gerald Ford was not elected in 1976, it meant my friend would leave the US Attorney's office and about same time I had a chance to join an insurance defense firm in Madison.

At the insurance defense firm, I tried all kinds of cases for various insurance companies. Most were serious, but some were fun – a mouse in the pop bottle case, a case involving an accident where a naked milk truck driver ran a stop sign on a Sunday morning and broadsided a car with eight people inside, a case involving the Frankenstein Monster from Universal Studios in California, and a case where the judge described the plaintiff, a high school kid, as "the clumsy bastard who cut off three of his fingers" in shop class. While I really enjoyed trying cases, trial work is a life of meeting all kinds of deadlines for discovery, motions, briefing and actual trial preparation resulting too often in an unpredictable work schedule. In 1980, by then having three young kids, and back in the Guard for the foreseeable future, I looked for a more "normal" civilian work life.

In 1980, I joined the law department of Clark Oil & Refining Corporation in Milwaukee. Clark had 1800 service stations in the Midwest, two refineries, and a pipeline. It was one of Wisconsin's largest companies in terms of revenues with almost a billion dollars of sales my first year. My first day with the company, a Milwaukee newspaper ran a business page headline "Clark Oil Sale Rumored". No sale was actually pending then but 2 ½ years later the company was sold and moved to St. Louis. My marriage in 1982 was going downhill at an increasing rate and my wife, not surprisingly, said she would not go with me to St. Louis. I was not interested in living that far from my kids and looked for, and found, a job with the Allis Chalmers Corporation Law Department also located in Milwaukee.

Four days before my start date in summer 1982, my new boss at Allis called me in and told me the Corporation had put a hiring freeze in place and I no longer had a job. The law department did hire me on a contract basis to research an issue for them which gave me time to get into a four-month Dept. of Defense course at Patrick AFB in Florida. Patrick is right on the Atlantic Ocean, has a great beach, golf course, tennis courts, great BOQs, and was everything an AFB should be. I saw a shuttle launch, and the DoD course itself was perhaps the best course I have ever attended. I arrived back in Milwaukee shortly before Christmas and on Christmas Eve, my almost boss at Allis Chalmers called and said the law department now had the authority of the Allis Chalmers CEO himself to hire a lawyer, and was I by chance interested. I was, and went to work for the corporate law department on January 3, 1983. Three months later the lawyer that hired me, fired me, and hired me again, came into my office with some good news and some bad news. The good news was he had gotten me into Allis Chalmers Credit Corporation and the bad news was the corporate law staff was being cut and being the newest lawyer, that was me. I enjoyed my time at Allis Chalmers and Allis Chalmers Credit Corporation, but when it became clear the entire Allis group was going to fail, I started looking again. In 1985 was hired as an Assistant General Counsel by Wisconsin's largest banking organization, First Wisconsin Corporation. I also enjoyed my time with that organization until it was bought out 14 years later and the law department disbanded.

In case you are counting, from 1980-1998 I was on the corporate law departments at the demise of three of Wisconsin's largest corporations in three different fields – gasoline marketing, manufacturing, and banking. (So far, I have received no recognition for that remarkable feat.) In 1986 my long failing marriage of 20 years also finally came to an end. A few months later I met Sherry who had just finished a 17 year marriage. We married two years later and have been together for going on 35 years. A neighbor, whose own marriage ended after 35 years and is trying to decide if he should risk it again, remarked that Sherry and I are, "as happy as two clams," and we are - if that is a good thing, not knowing exactly how happy clams are.

My final civilian job was with a small law firm started by lawyers that had been in large firms but wanted to practice law and not spend as much time administering a law firm. The firm was a great place to work, good lawyers, good staff, good clients, and nice people. I was with that firm beginning in 1998 for over 15 years gradually working less and less until a couple years into my 70's.

In the Guard, I had great assignments. I got into Wisconsin's general support artillery brigade in 1980, was commander of a battalion of 155 self-propelled howitzers starting in 1982 for over four years and five annual trainings. Followed that with three years as the brigade operations officer, and followed that with three years as brigade commander. I spent my final three years at state HQs while the State decided if they needed me in one of its administrative O-7 assistant adjutant general positions. I didn't like the HQ assignment much which was probably apparent to everyone. The State lost one of its general positions when I came up for promotion so the lone O-7 position went to another colonel. The State made the right choice.

However, during those last three years, I attended the Army War College and really enjoyed it. On graduation, I received a writing award for an independent study paper I wrote comparing the strategy of the American Rebels during the Revolution to that employed by the NVA/VC during our war. The College suggested I work on the paper some more and submit it for publication in one of the Army periodicals. I did and it was rejected. Still, I am sure Carl von Clausewitz of *On War* fame would have agreed with me and my conclusions. Too bad he died in 1831. I might have become a respected military scholar.

In summary, no serious complaints with either my military or civilian careers, bad first marriage but a great second marriage, great kids and grandkids, a mildly psychotic dog but small so almost harmless – a very good life. The Clarinda reunion remains one of my favorite events every year. Also, I remain very proud of the 61st pilots and families, who built and continue to support the Bong Son library.

Dick Easterwood:
Went to Oklahoma State University. Was in ROTC – flight training. Enlisted in local reserve. Went on active duty and was 2nd lieutenant. Worked for an oil company in Houston for 1 year. Went to flight school. Got married and got orders for the 61st AHC. Went to Detroit during the riots as a sr. lieutenant. Was an intelligence officer and sent to Jungle Survival School. Was operations officer for the 61st in Nam- 3 years active duty. Worked for Shell for an independent oil subsidiary company. Retired in 2007. Married in 1966 and still married. 2 kids, 2 grandkids, and 1 on the way. Have a place in Colorado. Was in the reserves for 30 years. Retired as lieutenant colonel. 10 moves, was in Nam 1967- 68.

Frank Brisker:
Graduated high school – liked to fly – flunked out of college – enlisted. Went to flight school. Was at Ft. Polk – was in the first group to infuse into the 61st. After Nam went back to Rucker. Got out and flew helicopters for a coal company. Flew airplanes from 1985-2003. Moved to Cincinnati. Retired. Bounced around doing contract work for 10 years, flying. Flies Hueys places – next month going to be in Gettysburg to give free rides in the Huey. Was in Nam 1968-69. Married for 47 years. 4 kids, 4 grandkids. Was in the Army 3 ½ years. Was in the national guard 22 years. Was in the inactive reserve for 15 years. 3 moves, 30 years in the same job--flying.

Dany Pennington:
Lived in Guam as a kid, then in Virginia. Parents divorced twice. Left home at 16. Parents were pilots. Bought airplanes, got married. Father-in-law said they needed pilots so I joined up and went to Ft. Wolters. Went to Nam on a boat with the 61st. Was in Nam 1967-68, 2 kids, 1 grandkid and 1 on the way. In the Army several years, married once. Worked construction. Was chief pilot for private company flying for Saudi Arabian royalty.

Dany, a highly respected, superb pilot in Vietnam, wrote an article which was published in the Aviator, Vietnam Helicopter Pilot's news magazine. It was about Sam Kyle's amazing rescue of a LRRP team which I have alluded to earlier. His description is much better than mine. He's also written a semi-fictional account of a combat episode with the 61st AHC in Vietnam.

Wayne Henning:
Played football for Nebraska. Wanted to fly jets. Had an appointment to the Air Force/Navy Academy. Went to college and then the Army to fly. Flew Hueys – went to the 61st where the action was. Drew straws and that's where I was sent. Came back and was an instructor at Wolters. Got an A&P, aircraft and powerframe, license and worked for Goodyear Rubber Company. Crop duster, bought helicopter – parted ways with partner. Had my own business. 1985 joined new Guard unit. Sold business. In Omaha flying EMS – still flying. Married in flight school, divorced. Married again and widowed 2 years

ago. Married again to Helen. 2 kids, (5 with 1st wife), 14 grandkids, 3-5 moves, in Nam 1969-70.

Pete Swanz:
Was drafted and volunteered for airborne. Went to airborne cook school – applied for flight school. Had knee surgery – sent to 61st. Loved gunships. Worked closely with LRRP's. Came back to the States and discharged. Once home, drank/partied – sold auto parts. Married – had 3 kids (daughter died) – have 2 sons. Was married 17 years. Had a job in Florida, then unemployed, in Ready Reserve, then active duty in 1991 until Saudi War was ended. Worked in accounting/training/Department of Corrections. When 62, classified by VA as totally disabled. 2 grandkids, in the army 12 years, 9 moves, was in Nam 1968-69. Live in Florida.

Kevin Campbell:
Graduated Nebraska-went to 3 semesters of college-flunked out. Was told to fly helicopters. Went to Plei Ku-same area as 61st. With the 155th AHC, (Assault Helicopter Co.) Stagecoach 23. Was in Battle of Dak To - Tet '68. Isolated company. Airforce gunships and 6 Nam policeman fought it out. While on R&R got married. Transferred to Hawaii-wife got out of the Army when she got pregnant. Back to Nam to the 155thAHC. Went to Ban Me Thuot . Needed experienced pilots in Nam. Spent 6 months flying VIP's around. Extended in the Army and then got riffed out (position eliminated) of the Army. Had 2 kids-went to Montana – School of Forestry. Joined National Guard for 5 years – CW3. Turned down Ft. Bragg. Went to Ft. Rucker for 3 years. Then Alaska.

Retired out of Army. Then flew for Air Force. Gave up job; wanted airplane job. Flew Cessna 337 in Africa flying surveillance. Took job in Omaha. Flew with Wayne H.– still flying. 2 kids, 2 grandkids, in the army 23 years, 14-15 moves, was in Nam '67-'68 and '70-'71. *Kevin was actually in another unit but has attended our reunions in Iowa at Chief Zogleman's.*

Lyle Real:
Real Flying Times-I never grew up dreaming of flying. As a young boy growing up in Nebraska on a family farm, the nearest airport was 28 miles from my home. My first flight was in a J3 cub on an Easter Sunday when I was between 8-10 years old. I had 5 classmates in grade school and that grew to 8 for HS. After graduating from HS, with no funds for college, it was a matter of time before being drafted.

I enlisted in the U.S. Army April 1968. Basic training was at Ft. Polk, LA. It was the first time I left the state of Nebraska. 10 weeks later I arrived at Ft. Wolter, TX, to begin WORWAC 69-3 with 277 other candidates. I was one of the last pilots to solo from my flight, as my instructor wasn't one to push you out of the nest early. During the phase two of training at Wolters, I was always assigned to fly with some of the other pilot's that were having difficulties no matter how much I pleaded with the instructor to fly with someone else.

Then off to Ft. Rucker and for some reason, I was able to get the hang of instrument flying. However, I wasn't chosen to receive a standard instrument rating. Graduated Flight School March, 1969, and was lucky to be assigned to the 61st AHC. It proved to be the beginning of good things that happened to me for the rest of my Army career. One of the best things about my time at the 61st was the fact that assignments were based on the best person for the job, regardless of one's rank. I was able to become AC after the required 90 days in country, and 2 months later made IP for the 1st platoon. I was wounded and sent back to the US in April, 1970.

After recovery from my wounds, I was assigned to the 1st Inf Div., Ft. Riley, KS. During my time at Ft. Riley, I taught myself instrument flying and gained my instrument rating at the KS National Guard. We did not have an instrument examiner at Ft Riley at that time. Additionally, I began working on my fixed wing ratings via the GI Bill. As the Army moved to require all Army Aviators to have an instrument rating, I was chosen to go to Ft. Rucker and attend the Instrument Examiners Course, then returned to Riley and set up and ran the instrument qualification course for the Post. As you may know, part of the 1st Inf. Div. mission was to return to Germany for an annual exercise called Reforger. That is one of the most challenging jobs for Army aviators. Leaving an area you know like the back of your hand, and now being placed in a country where you cannot even pronounce the name of the place you are supposed to fly to.

April, 1973, was assigned to Ft. Rucker for CH-54 qualification and then the Advanced course. Following that assigned to the Special Forces in Thailand. The week I arrived in Thailand, the Thai government asked the Special Forces (Green Berets) to leave the country. I was able to get the Army to change my assignment to fly U-21s for the Joint Causality Resolution Center. Another lucky opportunity for someone who never went to the Army fixed-wing qualification course. Returning from Thailand, I was assigned to the 478th Heavy Lift Co. at Ft. Benning, GA. While at Benning, I became an instructor pilot in both the CH-54 and the Post fixed-wing aircraft.

And now off to Germany. My first assignment was to the 330 EWC Guard Rail Co. flying RU-21 H aircraft. This was absolutely the worst assignment of my Army career. I was able to change assignments to the 207th Avn. Co. a year later and was the Standardization Instructor Pilot for all of Germany for the next four years. This was a great assignment, flying both C-12 and UH-1 all over most of Europe. After five years in Germany, it was time to return to the US.

Returned to Ft. Belvoir, VA, where I was the C-12 Standardization Pilot for Davison Army Airfield. As time went by, I was sent to the C-21 qualification course, which was a US Air Force run program. The Army was to get a Lear 35 jet. I never flew it, as it was held up in the court system for years, but did eventually come to the Army. In 1988 the Army received the last two Gulfstream 3 aircraft off the assembly line in Savannah, GA. I was chosen to become the first Standardization Instructor Pilot for the new unit.

Finally, it was time to go seek fame and fortune elsewhere. Retired from the U.S. Army June, 1990. July, 1990 to December, 1991 flew for Mobil Oil Corp, at Dulles, VA. Gulfstream 3 and Hawker aircraft. February, 1992-November, 1993 worked for British Aerospace as a training captain for Hawker aircraft and helped develop the Hawker simulator. November, 1993-May,1995 flew a Hawker aircraft for a private family that had homes in Key Largo, FL, and Pebble

Beach, CA. Was captain and check airman for Av. Jet in the Hawker aircraft. June, 1995-June, 1998 flew Gulfstream aircraft for Av. Jet as captain and check airman in Burbank, CA, July,1998- March, 2005 flew Gulfstream 3 and Lear 55 aircraft at Spirit Airport, as Chief Pilot and Aviation Manager.

June, 2005 until December, 2020 flew for Net Jets, Inc as captain for Gulfstream, Phenom and Cessna Latitude. My last landing was December 17, 2020, at Boeing Field, WA, on a dark, windy and rainy night. Finished with 22,300 hours without an accident. Not bad for a farm kid from Nebraska!

Gordon Wax:
Born in Montana. Joined the reserve 3 months before graduating. Worked as a cowboy. Went to basic training -crew chief. Assigned to the 335th Assault Helicopter Co, then to 61st. Went over on a ship. A peak experience occurred when he was pondering death and a spiritual feeling came over him that stays with him today. Home from Nam took an A & P license, got private and commercial/CFI pilot's licenses and ratings. Got into accounting program and passed CPA exam. Worked for government for 8 years. Was in the CIA regional office – saw the stealth fighter. Installed space applications software for GPS system. Installed software across the country until 1995. Has 2 houses-California and Montana. Works as a CPA in winter, farms during the summer. Reads history, maintains the 61st AHC website. Was in Nam 1968-'70 as tech inspector. Was in army 2 years, 9 months, 2 days. Married twice/divorced – 3 sons, no grandkids, 12 moves.

Every year for 12 years we, the 61st AHC, have had a reunion of pilots, crew members, spouses, ex-wives, girlfriends, veterans and interested parties held in College Springs and Clarinda, Iowa. It's hosted by Chief Zogleman, his wife, Kathy, and their family of two daughters, their husbands and sons. Plus his sister Diane, who contributed selflessly to the Library and his sister Deb, who along with husband Craig, have been mighty strong supporters of the 61st reunions. They provided "Welcome Home" posters and banners for our reunions. Most Vietnam veterans were never formally recognized for their service, until after 911, and this has made a really positive lasting impression on all involved. Their daughter, Michelle Hilliard, is in charge of the alternative school, "Complete High School Maize" that they started and the students created the posters and banners. We loved it!

Last year, at our reunion, we honored Meridith Claus Beck, who had been the American Red Cross Field Hospital Director on board the USS Repose hospital ship which was stationed off the coast of Vietnam during '68-'69. The Red Cross, among many other services, provided a connection with a combat soldier's family if they were wounded or needed to resolve family issues, enabling them to get word to their wives and loved ones. Meridith's uniforms, photos, Red Cross flag from the Repose, cruise book, memos, military orders, award certificates and memorabilia of her service are housed in the Vietnam Center and Archive at Texas Tech University in Lubbock, TX. Vietnam veterans can have their stories recorded through personal interviews and stored in the archives by contacting the Center, www.vietnam.ttu.edu. Researchers and historians will then have access to actual Vietnam War veterans' experiences and memorabilia, and be able to advise future policymakers of the proper course of action, we hope.

But this year, 2022, we won't have a reunion due to multiple injuries and operations undergone by the Chief. We are all approaching the 80s, too. So maybe we will all catch a second wind, the 80s are the new 60s or something like that and resume the reunions, or we won't. Here are some of the short bios of other veterans who have attended:

Jeff Lux:
Actually, Jeff's not a veteran, but came from a family of veterans. Jeff is an accomplished musician and former member of the band, *Kansas*, who attends our reunions. He plays multiple instruments and entertains us with songs of the Vietnam era and blues, rhythm, rock and roll and original creations. We dance and sing along. Here's Jeff's interesting background: Mom graduated from college at age 15. She worked in DC for FBI at age 16. She played music. He, Jeff, became an electrified musician. Born in 1953 and was serious musician at age 10. Been in bands ever since. Several bands with Steve Walsh. Member of the band "Kansas." Lived in band house in Topeka. Got $1 per day. Married 39 years, 3 kids. Got into teaching by accident when they needed a substitute. Been teaching 12 years.

Henry Laurent:

Graduated high school in 1969. Joined army – wanted to jump out of planes. Dad was in army for 26 years. Went to airborne school at Ft. Leonard Wood. Was infantry airborne. It was dangerous being in this. Signed up for special ops – disbanded as it was too rough. Went to Special Forces school. Was in Nam 1971-'72. Was in the Green Berets with a 6-man team finding MIA's. Trained Cambodians. Got out of the Army then got into the Reserve. Worked for utility company. 6 months in the Amy, then 6 months out. Was in 26 years. Was in the First Gulf war. Was in Kuwait to train the Kuwait army. Burned badly and was in the hospital for 2 ½ years. At age 42 was permanently disabled. Also PTSD. Married once for 4-5 months, then married in the 80s again and divorced in Kansas City in the same house. Collects cars – 3 kids, no grandkids.

Mike Meyer:

Went to high school with Henry – graduated high school and went to flight school. Lost deferment and got drafted. Basic training in Ft. Leonard Wood. Eyes not good enough to be a pilot but okay for crew chief. Was assistant county clerk and volunteered for Nam. Was in the 56th medivac unit. Served as door gunner. Worked recovery in 3 corps. After Nam married best friend's wife – still married. Wife is a professional singer with 4 Grammy's. Went to college – got a BA in economics – trading commodities. Own brokerage firm. Retired. Delivered medical supplies for 5 years to Nam. Does programs to support military families. Started a coalition to address issues that VA doesn't take care of. 2 kids, 4 grandkids,

Was in Nam 1970-'71. In Army 2 years, 1 month, 2 days, 3 moves.

<u>Larry Cooperider:</u>
Went to college – flunked out – got into drag racing. Was drafted and went to Nam in armored unit. Was a security guard in Cam Ranh Bay. Back from Nam, bought a farm in Ohio. Bought a GT car – sold it and son got it back for him. Married for 17 years – divorced for 22 years, 4 kids, 5 grandkids, 1 move, was in Nam 1969-'70.

<u>Summary</u>: *Mighty fine bunch of folks who spent a considerable portion of their lives in service to their country*. That one year in combat in Vietnam left a deeply imprinted memory on all who were there. Often, that memory was conflicted by the fact that this dangerous duty was ignored and/or berated by the general public, students, clergy, college professors, businesses, and just about everybody.

Once the Pentagon Papers came out and we saw how we had been duped by Johnson, McNamara and Westmoreland into believing this was a winnable, justifiable war against communism, our efforts seemed negligible at best, regrettable at the least, and unfortunate and unnecessary. This led to lots of PTSD and internal strife for the veteran. Even today with our ongoing wars in the Middle East, returning veterans have a much higher than average suicide rate.

Another opinion is that the U.S. justifiably impeded the expansion of communism into neighboring countries by becoming involved militarily in Vietnam. Probably so, thus our efforts weren't totally in vain, but I think we could have done better by diplomatically pursuing a course of reconciliation through agricultural, medical programs and business development. The Vietnamese are reasonable people and not religious zealots.

Another interesting point investigated by Dr. Bill Gondring, Commander, USN surgeon, and cousin-in-law, is that the VC and NVA that he treated were not familiar with the term "communism" as motivation to form a government. They just wanted to drive the Americans out of their country and unify South and North Vietnam.

Related summary:
We, my wife Pat and I, have just returned from attending the funeral of a Vietnamese friend. The beautiful, exuberant, talented singer, mother and friend, Mai Le, had donated money to our Library Learning Center (LLC) in Bong Son. She was a waitress at the Golden Dragon restaurant in McPherson, KS, and when she heard me talking about the LLC she felt moved to offer a contribution. I was moved, as here was a lady working two jobs to support her children in college, and yet she digs deep in her purse and donates to the education of the Vietnamese children she left behind in Vietnam. It seemed so remarkable to me; she came all the

way from Vietnam to die in McPherson, KS, my hometown, while I and my brother-in-law and others had gone all the way to Vietnam not to die. All of us didn't make it back. Two of my hometown friends and a fraternity brother were killed in service to the dubious cause of protecting the Vietnamese from their countrymen and brothers. A blithe spirit like Mai Le, the empathetic, altruistic fun-loving Lady of the Lake could change the world if only grace and beauty were valued as highly as fear, aggression, and greed, or whatever it is that turns our heads away from compassion and family to violence and brutality.

And then came the amazing lesson: "Love is stronger than death." Mai Le's service was conducted by a Methodist lady pastor who asked us all to pray with her in our own particular belief and way. Then she reminded us that although one passes on, love overpowers death as we recall and recreate the beauty of existence.

Later that evening as we attended a wedding reception for our dear friends' son who had met online and developed a lasting unity with a lovely Russian woman, we heard from Rumi, a Sufi mystic quote that, "Love supports the Milky Way and the universe." I like to think in this way; as the power of our minds to organize perception is so imaginative and creative. Meditation and prayer may save us all, or, may prayer and meditation save us all. Save us from what, you might say. Well, as Pogo, the philosophical cartoon character exclaimed, **"We have met the enemy, and they are us."**

Appendix A: National Vietnam War Museum

In July of this year, 2022, many Vietnam veterans, pilots, crew members, and representatives of all the armed forces gathered in Mineral Wells, Texas, for the dedication of the National Vietnam War Museum. Mike Myer, member of the board, invited Chief Zogleman and me to attend. Ft. Wolters, near Mineral Wells, was the Primary Helicopter Training School during the Vietnam War era, and almost all helicopter pilots went through a 4-month stage there. Flying over the Texas prairie and farm land, and watching the Brazos River snake through the semi-arid landscape, seemed a strange prelude and preparation for the steamy jungles of Vietnam. Overall, the U.S. military used nearly 12,000 helicopters in Vietnam, of which more than 5,000 were destroyed. (www.vvmf.org)

Jim Messinger, who along with several others ramrodded the inception of the museum, introduced the keynote speaker, Troy Evans. Troy is a well-respected actor who has appeared in both the movies and in TV series since returning from his tour in Vietnam in 1970.

I expected some sort of rah-rah speech about how we fought bravely in Vietnam for God and our country, the American way, democracy, capitalism, baseball, Mom and apple pie, which we did, but Troy, bless his heart, delivered this honest and inspiring message:

Troy Evans:

National Vietnam War Museum Address

Thanks for the honor of making this presentation. You may know that the great writer and hero, Joe Galloway, had agreed to speak today, but unfortunately, he has passed. I would like to honor him with a quote from Shakespeare's *Henry V* that Joe also used in his book, *We Were Soldiers Once, and Young:* "We few, we happy few, we band of brothers; for he today who sheds his blood with me shall be my brother."

I believe a number of you are pilots, and I want to give a special thank you to all of you for your courage and support that saved innumerable lives of ground pounders like me.

My father, Leo. was a pilot. He flew the P-51 Mustang off Iwo Jima in WWII. On April 12, 1945, he flew the first Tokyo raid of WWII. Aug. 9, he flew to NAGASAKI. Aug. 12, he escorted 274 bombers to OSAKA. They were told that the Japanese were surrendering and that the mission would be cancelled as soon as the papers were signed. Five minutes after they dropped the payload, they received word that the war was over. They had killed over 100,000 civilians as the peace treaty was being signed. Dad regretted that for the rest of his life.

Jump cut to 1968, I'm a young Sgt. in Viet Nam. My unit, 2/22 Mechanized Infantry of the 25th Infantry Division, had been sent into the Iron Triangle in hopes of finding an NVA battalion that was rumored to be in the area. We had spent the night there with zero enemy contact. We set out in the morning to sweep the area around our camp. We had a dog handler, and his German shepherd assigned to us to help with this sweep. We knew the Dogman as he had been with us on several other occasions. I took a photo of him as we set out that morning since we knew this was his last day in the field. Tonight, he would fly to Tan Son Nhat airport to prepare to ship back to the States. Our CO was a wonderful man named Cpt. Dan Makita.

We were set up next to a clearing and we started across it towards the wood line with the Dogman about 50 yards ahead of us. I will never know why the dog didn't alert until he was about 5 feet from the bunker. As soon as he did, they hit them both with machine gun fire, the Dogman in both legs and the dog in the chest. The Dogman was young, and tough, and brave, and smart and knew instantly that the only way he could survive was to throw himself on top of that ground level enemy bunker, which he did and pulled the dog with him. He started yelling, "I'm hit! I'm Hit! I'm hit, but I'm OK. Come get me you MF-ers." The dog was yelling too. A desperate howl that I will never forget.

We now had all three platoons pinned down and no ability to put fire on the bunker because they were stuck right on top of it, continuing to yell, and howl. Two guys on the right flank tried to cover each other as they rushed the bunker, and were cut down like spring wheat. The first platoon medic tried to creep around to the left and was shot in the right eye. People continued to get hit by the second, as we had no effective way to return fire.

Captain Makita was appalled that he had misjudged the situation so badly. He grabbed a canvas bag of grenades and tried to Audi Murphy it up the center of the field. I was his RTO and his absence left me essentially in charge. He made it about halfway to the bunker before the surgeon on that 51 caliber took his leg off at the hip. I can still see the leg floating above his head. It looked like ballet. He fell into the only low spot in that entire clearing which allowed him to get his shirt off, tie off his stump, and survive.

I think everything I've described so far took place in less than two minutes. I was a 21-year-old Buck Sgt. My CO was down. I was surrounded with dead and wounded. The dog still howled, and the Dogman was still yelling, "Come and get me you Sons of Bitches. I'm going home!" I happened to be carrying an M-72 LAW. It is basically a light, disposable bazooka. I thought about it for about 1/10 of a second and I popped it open and fired. That was it. It was over. I killed that machine gunner. I killed the dog, and I killed the Dogman. I was the man of the hour, and the Dogman, well, the Dogman went home five days early, in a plastic bag.

What connects my dad's story and mine is just this: each of us, father and son, had done our best to fight the good fight, to serve when needed. To do the right thing. And even though what we did was the best thing we could do in that moment— it was still hideous. My dad spent the rest of his life as a father, a successful and well-liked small businessman in Kalispell, MT. When he passed, I don't think a dozen people in town knew he'd been a fighter pilot.

When my brother, Todd, was about 14, he heard a terrible sound in the middle of the night. He thought our dog was dying. He found Dad in a corner of the basement — wailing. Todd was horrified. "Dad, what's wrong?" Leo said, "Todd, I don't even know how many people I killed."

Let's stop putting young men and women in positions where when they do the very best they can, they can't live with the result. **Wouldn't it be great if this was the *last* war museum?** Unfortunately, we are already 3 or 4 wars behind.

I was doing some yard work in LA and a four-year-old who was visiting a neighbor approached me. "Hey mister, do you want to know a secret?" Sure. "I'm going to be in a wedding. and I'm going to carry the wedding ring— and I will be wearing silver shoes!" Wow, do you know any other secrets? — He looked me over and said, "I'm Batman." Wow, how did you find out you were Batman? That is when he gave me "the look." You know, the, "is something wrong with your head?" look.   Then he told me: **"I've got the shirt."**

I've thought about this, and realized the reason that I was able to step out of this world, and into the world of mortal combat was: **I had the shirt.** We all did. Every person here that served, put on **the shirt,** and showed up. And thousands have put on **the shirt** one last time and laid in a box while their family wept. Let's try to stop that. In his book Joe Galloway quotes US Grant, "**There has never been a time that some way could not be found to prevent the drawing of the sword.**" Let's look for that way.

In WWI, 1919, there was a heroic British Anglican priest named Jeffrey Studdert Kennedy. He rescued many wounded men and was known for sitting and talking with them till they died. He wrote this poem:

Waste

Waste of muscle, waste of Brain,
Waste of Patience, waste of Pain,
Waste of Manhood, waste of Health,
Waste of Beauty, waste of Wealth,
Waste of Blood, waste of Tears,
Waste of youth's most precious years,
Waste of ways the saints have trod,
Waste of Glory, Waste of God.
WAR!

I'm going to give my dad the last word. When he passed, he left two items secreted in the back of his desk drawer. One was a picture of his fighter squadron on the eve of the first mission to Japan off Iwo Jima signed by each of those pilots. He also had a piece of Japanese paper money signed by each of those men, and these precious items were folded inside a piece of paper on which my dad had copied, in pencil, Shel Silverstein's poem, Hug o' war.

Hug o' War

I will not play at tug o' war.
I'd rather play at hug o' war,
Where everyone hugs
instead of tugs,
Where everyone giggles
And rolls on the rug.
Where everyone kisses,
And everyone grins,
And everyone cuddles,
And everyone wins.

We can all appreciate those sentiments and wish for a more sane and cogent approach to foreign and domestic affairs in the future.

This morning in my English as a Second Language (ESL) Zoom class with teen-age Vietnamese students living between Saigon/HCMC and Vung Tau, I was reminded that perhaps our trials and tribulations are not for aught after all. If life were perfect and we lived in a peaceful utopian society, we would tend toward slothfulness and apathy as everything was always good and plentiful. However, faced with daily contingencies as we are, our character is continually challenged to become better and brighter to insure our survivability. So, the ups and downs of modern life are the best of all possible worlds. **It's sort of like flying a helicopter; Whop, Whop, Whop, do your best, drive carefully, and have a good time.**

Appendix B: Now how about some photos:

    This is Chief Zogleman and Captain Embers at the dedication of the Bong Son Lucky Star Blazers Library Learning Center Dec. 9, 2011, rainy season. The Library Learning Center is in the background. We've been back every year, expect during the Covid-19 exclusionary period.

Chief Zogleman preparing to go or just getting back from another gunship mission in 1969. Looks like he's expended all the rockets from the two rocket pods. Each holds 17, 2.75" rockets. A 40 mm grenade launcher is mounted on the front of this "B" model Huey. He's wearing the new Nomex flight outfits we got to replace the former gray cotton flight suits that we initially wore and then the cotton jungle fatigues and plastic mesh jungle boots. We wore the Nomex uniform and all leather boots as a safety precaution as those items were more fire resistant in case of an emergency.

Capt. Embers in the aircraft commander's pilot seat with a trusty crew chief who has maintained and armed the aircraft with 2.75 rockets and 7.62 mini gun ammo. Note the miniguns have six barrels and fire more than 4,000 rounds per minute. The crew chief does all the daily regular maintenance on the aircraft. There are hundreds of moving parts on a helicopter, fluid levels to top off, and many items to attend to, including making sure that the "Jesus nut" that attaches the main rotor blade to the main mast is secure.

One of our slick (lift) platoon Huey's poised for action, in a revetment to protect it from mortar and rocket attack, 1969. Occasionally we received damaging mortar fire at night and more than once "sappers" penetrated the perimeter and tried to place satchel charges near the helicopters.

Formation flying over the Bong Son plains. We are airlifting troops of the 173rd Airborne Brigade over the mountains west of LZ English into the An Lao Valley.

A single ship Huey slick carrying a six member LRRP team for an insertion in the mountains. Their feet and legs are hanging out the side of the Huey. The LRRP's performed reconnaissance and ambush missions. And then would call us in the middle of the night to come and pick them up. A very hairy scary mission!

The view looking at the mountains to the west of LZ English on a typical fog shrouded morning. Beautiful rice paddies and coconut palms provided agricultural bounty and sustenance for the local populace. Peanuts and wood furniture are also produced in the area now.

The Library; we originally wanted to call it the 61st Assault Helicopter Library Learning Center, but the local People's Committee objected to any memorialization of the American soldiers who had fought there. They didn't understand the historical significance of a former combatant, especially a helicopter unit, returning to build an edifice dedicated to peaceful resolution of conflict. I can see their point in the "small" picture, but in the "big" picture it is a colossal effort to establish a network of communication and relationships that could lead to greater understanding and cooperation. *Always the optimist.*

Le, our interpreter, wife Pat, me, and a People's Committee representative, singing a traditional friendship song in Vietnamese. Trish (Pat) learned the song in Vietnamese. A People's Committee representative, a member of the executive branch of the government attends and monitors all official functions. Or maybe he was a school official. In any case, we all had a good time!

Kids and their teacher, Thuy in an ESL (English as a Second Language) class at the Ross Worley English School. An example of one of the spin-offs of our involvement with the LOVP, Library of Vietnam Project. Thuy, whose professional ESL teacher's name is "Joel" has a long list of parents wanting to get their kids into her classes. Her students regularly compete successfully in regional and national English contests

Some of the Phu Hoa Catholic Orphanage kids in Quang Ngai. The big kids, they can stay until they are 17, were in school. The 61st AHC gave the children's home 9 computers during the COVID crisis in 2021 so that they could study online. Contrary to what you might think, being in this orphanage is not a bad deal. These kids get regular meals, health care, education up to 12th grade, and religious training. Khanh, our semi-adopted daughter that I'm holding, now 14, has learned to play the organ for mass.

In 2018, the logo and call sign of the 61st Assault Helicopter Company slicks, the "Lucky Stars" was adopted by the Army Aviation School helicopter pilot instructional unit at Ft. Rucker. What an honor!

Epilogue:

And why not include a song! The following poem-song, awaiting a melody, came to me on April Fool's Day a few years ago. It goes by various titles; "Hold Your Composure," subtitled "Prairie Wisdom", and now "Helicopter Heroes". We are heroes in that we see the wisdom and necessity of living a life of love and compassion, hard as it may be to say it and do it.

Hold Your Composure ©

Well, I was cruisin' along, mindin' my own bidnass',
When Chaos loomed and flew in my windas',
I turned to discern what had happened to me,
But it was too late, I could plainly see.
Fate had caught me at a turn in the road,
'n I couldn't cut back to try and even the load.
I was goin' over the edge, fallin' free.....

Now the only difference between fallin' and flyin'
Is you got some wings, so I started tryin'.
I spread my arms and controlled my breath,
Started flappin' my wings, but I was headed towards Death!
Then in the back of my mind, a phrase came forth,
If things are amiss and you're all alone,
Take time to consider how to get back home.

Hold your composure, don't panic and shout,
Hold your composure, don't let it fall out.
Hold your composure and proceed with a grin,
Things gotta change, like the weather and wind.

Well I was free fallin' over the edge of the cliff,
Tumbling upside down, eyes to the sky, saw a sign drift by.
It said, "Skateboarders Delight, turn right".
Wrenched around, to see the ground rushin' up to me;
I reached the bottom of the perigee,
And I was slung back up to the other side.
This wasn't death, and I hadn't died.
I was scootin' along on a skateboard slide!

Hold your composure, don't get carried away,
Hold your composure, hear what I say,
Hold your composure & look for some love,
It'll come to you, on the wings of a dove.

Originally, back in 1969 when I first told Chief Zogleman that I was going to write about our adventures, I pictured a comic book or a graphic novel like a Japanese manga reader, or a video with the "whop, whop, whop" sound of Huey helicopter rotor blades introducing each episode, but this is what ensued.

We never imagined that this war experience would lead to international cooperation and friendship.

Truly Amazing!

October, 2022

Addendum:

1. I wrote to Gary Roush of the Vietnam Helicopter Pilots Association and asked about the ratio of hostile fire deaths to accidental deaths. He responded;

Hi Ken,

We have not investigated this thoroughly. Here is a quick back of the envelope estimate:

There were 2,167 total helicopter pilots who died in the Vietnam War from all services, including Air America and some South Vietnamese.
We have Army accident reports listing 736 killed in helicopter accidents and 916 from helicopter hostile fire events out of 1,891 total U.S. Army KIAs. The remaining 239 died from various causes, i.e. illness, on ground accidents, mortars/rockets, misadventure, etc.

Assuming the U.S. Army represents all services it would break down something like this:

48 percent hostile fire
40 percent accidents
12 percent other

Gary

At 02:07 PM 9/29/2022, Ken Embers wrote:
>Gary Roush, VHPA, Editor & Chairman, Membership Directory

2. According to research by The Vietnam Helicopter Pilots Association there were about 12,000 helicopters that served in the Vietnam War…..out of which 5,086 were destroyed.

3. I also did a little more research into the origins of "algebra" and found that Al Jabarra isn't a man's name, but the method of solving equations that was developed by Muhammed ibn Musa al-Khwarizmi, a 9th century Muslim mathematician and astronomer. He is known as the "father of algebra", a word derived from the title of his book, *Kitab al-Jabr*. His work was based on the method of equational notation used by the Egyptians around 2500 B.C. Wonder where they got it?

4. Charlie Jones was the former Big Red One enlisted man who became a warrant officer pilot and helped me navigate the intricacies of obtaining lumber, supplies and equipment for several operational missions in Vietnam. He retired as a Signal Corps Colonel, achieving distinction as the US Army Philippine Embassy representative, then returning to his hometown of Marksville, LA to teach secondary school, coach basketball, serve as high school principal, city council member and as CEO/president of Avoyelles Parish, LA.

About the author:

Ken Embers lives in Manhattan, KS. Future plans include returning to Vietnam to visit the 61st AHC Bong Son Lucky Star Blazers Library Learning Center, the Phu Hoa Orphanage in Quang Ngai, Joel and her students at the Ross Worley English School in Phu My near Vung Tau, and to continue teaching ESL on Zoom to Vietnamese high school students preparing for the IELTS, International English Language Test Survey.

Maps courtesy of Wikipedia.

Bong Son, the small village next to LZ English, is about 600 miles from Hanoi and 400 miles from Saigon (Ho Chi Minh City). LZ English was the long term, temporary staging area and home for the 61st AHC in 1968-69.

The Socialist Republic of Vietnam today, in relation to neighboring countries. Hanoi is the capital.

Made in the USA
Monee, IL
09 October 2023

44270770R10089